'The things
which I have
here before
promised, I will
perform and
keep. So help me
God.'

KINGS &

QUEENS

BRENDA AND BRIAN WILLIAMS

The photographs are reproduced by kind permission of: Alecto Historical Editions 23b; The Art Archive 38r, 93; Ashmolean Museum, Oxford 11l, 53r; From His Grace The Duke of Atholl's Collection, Blair Castle 77t; John Bethell 33b, 39; Bridgeman Art Library 22, 27b, 40, 41t, 42r, 45r, 51, 55r, 77b (detail), 82r, 83, 117, 34 (Bibliotheque Nationale, Paris), 15b (British Library), 85r (Forbes Magazine Collection, New York), 84 (Harris Museum & Art Gallery, Preston, Lancashire), 89b, 91b (Private Collections), 47t (Royal Holloway and Bedford New College, Surrey); Peter Brimacombe 85l, 115r; British Library 15t, 17t, 23t, 26t, 29b & t, 35t, 37l, 68b, 30t (Weidenfeld & Nicolson Archives); British Museum 27t, 36r, 94l, 106; Camera Press (photo by Cecil Beaton) 122; Collections/Liz Stares 44; John Crook 8; Steve Day 92; Dean and Chapter of Westminster 4, 5bl, 7tr, 31, 36l; Dean and Chapter, St George's Chapel (by Sidney Newbery) 46; The Duke of Roxburghe 68t; Dundee Art Galleries 97c; Edinburgh Photographic Library 69; English Heritage 104, 109; Mary Evans Picture Library 70b; Malcolm Fife 67t & b; Fine Art Photographic Library 58, 60; Fotomas 61t, 81; John Freeman 80r; Getty Images 108t; Tim Graham 102l, 125t; Sonia Halliday 28; Robert Harding 50, 62; Hatfield House FCr; Historic Scotland (Crown Copyright) 63b; HM Stationery Office (Crown Copyright) 5br, 7tl; Michael Holford 14, 16t & b, 17b, 18l, 19, 33t, 61b; Angelo Hornak 7b; Anwar Hussein 123b; Sandra Ireland 11r; Andrew Stewart Jamieson 48/49; Jarrold Publishing 5t, 6, 10, 13, 20, 24t, 26b, 35b, 37r, 45l, 55l, 70t, 90, 91t, 101t, 103, 113r, 116; Leeds Castle 54b; Serge Lemoine 124; Mansell Collection 108b; The Master and Fellows of Corpus Christi College, Cambridge 12, 63t; John Minoprio 125b; National Army Museum 95; National Galleries of Scotland 73l & r, 97t; National Gallery of Ireland 100; National Maritime Museum 78, 80l, 82l; National Portrait Gallery 43, 47b, 52, 57, 86t, 87, 94r, 120; National Railway Museum 107b; The National Trust 54t, 75t; The National Trust for Scotland (by D. MacGregor) 75b; John Norris 79; Palace of Westminster Collection 88; Popperfoto 115l, 121l; Private Collection/National Museums of Scotland 63c; Public Record Office 76; Robert Harding Picture Library 72; Royal Academy of Arts 118l; The Royal Collection © 2004, Her Majesty Queen Elizabeth II 24b, 32, 38l, 56t, 69r, 74, 86c, 89t, 96, 97b, 98, 99t & b, 101b, 102r, 107t, 110/111, 112, 118r, 119l & r, 121r; Scotland in Focus 65, 71t; Scottish National Portrait Gallery 69l, 71b; Kenneth Scowen 66; Sherborne Castle Estates 59l; Skyscan 25; Society of Antiquaries 56b; Topham Picture Source 114; University of Ghent 42l; V&A Picture Library 41b, 86b; Viscount de L'Isle 59r; Walker Art Gallery, Liverpool 53l; Andy Williams 113l.

The map on page 18 was created by Hans Van Well.

The crown motif was created by Andrew Stewart Jamieson.

The family trees were produced by Simon Borrough.

A CIP catalogue for this book is available from the British Library.

Published by:
Jarrold Publishing
Healey House, Dene Road, Andover, Hampshire, SP10 2AA
www.britguides.com

Set in Minion.
Printed in Singapore.

ISBN 1 84165 130 3   2/05

 Pitkin Guides is an imprint of Jarrold Publishing, Norwich.

CONTENTS

The Chapel of Henry VII, the Lady Chapel, was begun in Westminster Abbey in 1503 on the king's orders. It was planned as King Henry VI's burial-place, but it was Henry VII who was laid to rest here after he died in 1509.

The coat of arms of the sovereign, quartering the arms of England, Scotland and Ireland. The three lions were first used by Richard the Lionheart (1189–99).

FROM ALFRED THE GREAT in the 9th century to Elizabeth II in the 21st, the throne of England has been occupied by 56 very varied men and women as kings or queens. The separate reigns of princes of Wales ended in 1284 when Wales was annexed to the English Crown, and from 1603 the royal line of Scotland merged with that of England. Since then one monarch has reigned over all the United Kingdom.

Some of the rulers in this long line of succession occupied the throne for no more than a few months. Several spent little time in their kingdom, and one or two spoke hardly any English. The reigns of Henry VI and Edward IV alternated during the Wars of the Roses. There were kings who seized the Crown, like Richard III, and kings who won it on the battlefield, like Henry VII. Charles I lost the Crown, and his head. The boy-king Edward V never had the Crown, Edward VIII gave it back, while Elizabeth I and Victoria survived early anxieties to reign long and gloriously, setting the seal of their names on the ages they lived through.

In this long line of monarchs, spread across the twisting branches of an ancient family tree, are kings and queens who were saints or scholars, heroes or villains, martyrs or murderers. They were feared and fearsome, witty and wise, amiable and amorous, innocent and guileful, hated and loved. Each left a distinctive mark on the history of these islands, and on the lives of its people.

CORONATION OF A KING

The Litlyngton Missal, a treasure of Westminster Abbey, shows a coronation. The crown is a symbol of earthly power and the coronation a ceremony rich in worldly and spiritual symbolism.

SOVEREIGN'S ORB

The orb, symbol of Christianity over the world, is part of the regalia used since Charles II's coronation (1660). The ancient crowns and sceptres were destroyed after the execution of Charles I in 1649.

RULES OF SUCCESSION

Most of the abbey was built for Henry III between 1220 and 1272.
The two west towers were the last major features – designed by
Sir Christopher Wren and completed by Nicholas Hawksmoor in 1745.

THE POWER AND FUNCTIONS of the monarch have never ceased to evolve, and rules of succession have been flexed to suit the needs of the time or the demands of the ruler. The area, people and customs of the kingdom have also changed. So we cannot picture William the Conqueror wrangling with Parliament any more than we can imagine George IV leading his troops into battle.

WHERE REIGNS BEGIN

Christians have worshipped on the site of Westminster Abbey in London since at least AD 960, when a monastic community was set up beside the River Thames. In 1065, Edward the Confessor built a large church here, intending it to be his burial-place. Most of the abbey that we see today was built for Henry III between 1220 and 1272 (column-bases from Edward's church remain, below the west nave). Monarchs since William I in 1066 have been crowned in the abbey. Several – among them Henry V, Henry VII and Elizabeth I – are buried here.

ST EDWARD'S CROWN

Made for Charles II, this crown is used only at the coronation. It replaced the crown said to have been worn by Edward the Confessor.

The coronation of George IV in 1821, the most sumptuous crowning ceremony ever experienced by a British monarch. His estranged queen was denied access to Westminster Abbey.

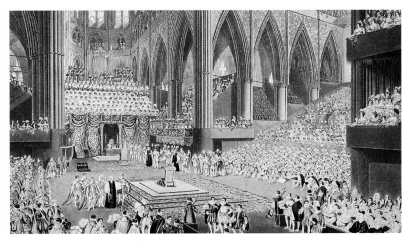

Just as the monarch's power and duties have changed, so have ideas about continuity. In ancient times, military leadership was a vital part of kingship, so it was thought best for the Crown to pass through the male line from father to son, or from brother to brother, or (as in Scotland in the early Middle Ages) to a king's most respected kinsman.

As the rules now stand, when a monarch has sons and daughters, the sons are first in line to inherit. The children (sons or daughters) of a monarch's eldest son take precedence over the second son, and he and his children take precedence over a third son, and so on. Only if a monarch has no living son – and no grandchildren through a son – will that monarch be succeeded by a daughter.

Queen Elizabeth II is descended from the native kings of Ireland as well as many generations of Scottish nobles. She also has links with the royal houses of France, Germany, Denmark and Spain, and – tracing that ancestry back into the mists of time – numbers among her remote forebears such historical notables as Attila the Hun, Alaric the Visigoth, crusader kings of Jerusalem and emperors of Byzantium, as well as several saints, alleged witches, poets and composers!

Many of us might claim similar ancestry, if we could delve far enough into the past. The descendants of Queen Victoria already number in the hundreds, and thousands of people could trace their ancestry back to a medieval king such as Edward III. Ancestry alone does not ensure the survival of a monarchy. It must adapt to change and earn respect through staying functional, while carrying on traditions that served previous generations well.

CORONATION CHAIR

The chair made on the orders of Edward I once enclosed the Scottish Stone of Scone. Since 1308 all English kings and queens have been crowned in this chair.

7

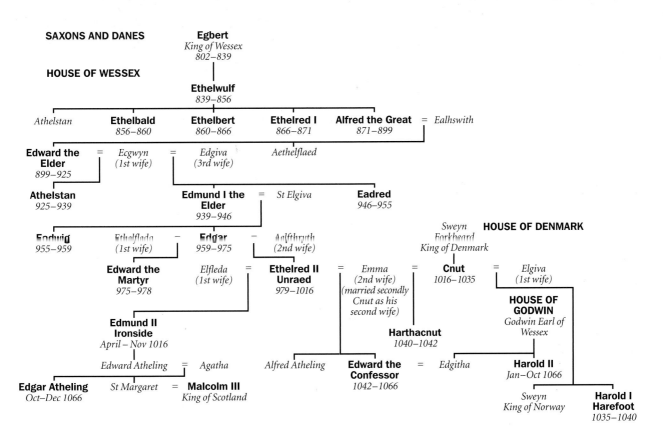

SAXONS AND DANES

HOUSE OF WESSEX

Egbert
King of Wessex
802–839

Ethelwulf
839–856

Athelstan | **Ethelbald** 856–860 | **Ethelbert** 860–866 | **Ethelred I** 866–871 | **Alfred the Great** 871–899 = *Ealhswith*

Edward the Elder 899–925 = *Ecgwyn (1st wife)* = *Edgiva (3rd wife)* | *Aethelflaed*

Athelstan 925–939 | **Edmund I the Elder** 939–946 = *St Elgiva* | **Eadred** 946–955

Sweyn Forkbeard King of Denmark **HOUSE OF DENMARK**

Eadwig 955–959 | *Ethelfleda (1st wife)* — **Edgar** 959–975 — *Aelfthryth (2nd wife)*

Edward the Martyr 975–978 | *Elfleda (1st wife)* = **Ethelred II Unraed** 979–1016 = *Emma (2nd wife) (married secondly Cnut as his second wife)* = **Cnut** 1016–1035 = *Elgiva (1st wife)*

HOUSE OF GODWIN
Godwin Earl of Wessex

Edmund II Ironside *April – Nov 1016*

Harthacnut 1040–1042

Edward Atheling = *Agatha* | *Alfred Atheling* | **Edward the Confessor** 1042–1066 = *Edgitha* | **Harold II** *Jan–Oct 1066*

Edgar Atheling *Oct–Dec 1066* | *St Margaret* = **Malcolm III** *King of Scotland*

Sweyn King of Norway | **Harold I Harefoot** 1035–1040

THE BRITISH MONARCHY BEGAN in an historical landscape very different from our experience. Although the land's geography and some of its place names may be the same, they belonged to a country that we would find unfamiliar. What we think of as the United Kingdom is a recent creation, in historical terms.

Immigrant Saxon warbands, settling after Roman control of Britain ended around 410, created the first English kingdoms. These existed as a constantly altering patchwork of warring tribal states over which first one, then another, gained supremacy. At various times, one ruler claimed ascendancy over all others. The historian Bede (d. 735) lists seven 'British rulers' or *Bretwaldas* – Aelle of Sussex (late 5th century), Ceawlin of Wessex, Ethelbert of Kent (d. 616), Raedwald of East Anglia (d. *c.* 625), and three kings of Northumbria: Edwin, Oswald and Oswy.

King Offa of Mercia (reigned 757–96) carved out a sizeable kingdom and claimed 'kingship of the English'.

In the 800s, the British Isles faced Viking attack. Resistance to these onslaughts helped unite the kingdoms of Wales, under Rhodri Mawr of Gwynedd (d. 878) and of Scotland, under Kenneth MacAlpin (reigned 843–60). In England, the kingdom of Wessex had risen to power in the early 9th century at the expense of Mercia and Northumbria. Viking attacks threatened to overwhelm all, including Wessex, the last free English kingdom. But the West Saxons had a stability in their ruling family that other English kingdoms lacked, through the four sons of King Ethelwulf. The last of these was Alfred, greatest of all Saxon kings, and the ruler whose life and reign begin the story of the kings and queens of England.

CATHEDRAL IN ALFRED'S ROYAL CAPITAL

In the 9th century, King Alfred made Winchester, a city with a pre-Roman history, his royal capital. The present cathedral, begun by the Normans in 1079, stands partly over an earlier Christian church, in which Saxon kings were crowned.

ALFRED THE GREAT (871–99)

ALFRED OF WESSEX, the only English ruler to hold the title 'Great', played a unique role in British history. Outstanding among Anglo-Saxon monarchs, he laid the foundations for the English kingdom as it existed into the Middle Ages.

MONARCH IN HIS CAPITAL

A statue of Alfred stands in Winchester, his capital and burial-place.

Alfred was the youngest son of Ethelwulf, King of Wessex from 839 to 856. He was a studious child, who showed promise, and in 855 spent a year on pilgrimage in Rome with his father. On his return, Ethelwulf made over the kingship to Alfred's brother Ethelbald, who was followed in succession by two more brothers, Ethelbert and Ethelred. At his brothers' side, young Alfred learned the skills of Wessex diplomacy and the harsher arts of the battlefield, fighting off Danish Vikings.

In 865 the Great Army of Norsemen, led by Ivar the Boneless and Halfdan, ravaged East Anglia, killing King Edmund, and invading Northumbria and Mercia. Only Wessex held out. When Ethelred died in 871, it was Alfred's turn to be king and defender of his people.

> '*He was a bountiful giver of alms … incomparably affable and pleasant to all men, and a skilful investigator of the secrets of nature.*'
>
> Asser, Welsh monk, writing of his friend and hero King Alfred

At one point, all seemed lost for Alfred, hiding out in the Somerset marshlands, but he recovered to thrash the Danes at Edington (Wiltshire) in 878. After this battle, the Danish leader Guthrum became a Christian, with Alfred as his godfather. The Treaty of Wedmore recognized Danish control east of a line from London to Chester. Known as the Danelaw, this region long retained a Scandinavian flavour in place names and law.

' ... amid wars and the frequent hindrances of this present life, the incursions of the pagans and his own daily infirmities of body, the king did not cease to carry on the government ... ' declared Asser.

Alfred read 'Saxon books', loved poetry and translated into English works by the Latin scholars Boethius and Augustine. He was also deeply religious: **'in the night he was wont to frequent the churches for prayers secretly'.**

ALFRED'S JEWEL

An elegant example of Saxon jewellery, made of gold and enamel, which may have belonged to King Alfred.

Alfred recaptured London from the Danes and reorganized the defence of his kingdom by creating fortified towns, or *burhs*, organizing the militia into a standing army, and building ships to patrol the coastline. When Vikings struck again in 890, the army and navy of Wessex were ready.

Far more than just a successful war-leader, Alfred devoted his energies to the well-being of his people – giving them education, fair laws and justice – so setting a model for the duties of a 'good king'. The unity of *Angelcynn*, 'the land of the English folk', was largely the king's vision. When Alfred died in 899, the kingdom and his mission passed to his son Edward.

NUNNAMINSTER RELIC

The Nunnaminster was a monastery in Winchester, founded by Alfred's queen Ealhswith in 903 and one of the centres of learning so valued by the king. The monastery was rebuilt in Norman times.

EDWARD THE ELDER TO EDWARD THE MARTYR: 899–978

EDWARD THE ELDER (899–925)

EDWARD THE ELDER (born *c.* 870) consolidated Alfred's kingdom, with the help of his elder sister, Aethelflaed. She married the king of Mercia and seems to have ruled that Midlands kingdom from 910 until her death in 917. Together, Edward and Aethelflaed inflicted a series of defeats on the Vikings. A renowned soldier, Edward was also keen to govern well; he 'used books frequently' and improved the coinage. On his death in 925, his son Athelstan (born *c.* 895) succeeded him.

ATHELSTAN AND
ST CUTHBERT

King Athelstan, a keen collector, presents a copy of Bede's works to St Cuthbert.

ATHELSTAN (925–39)

The royal house of Wessex reached a highpoint under Athelstan, *Rex Totius Britanniae* ('King of all Britain'). His defeat of allied Scots, Welsh and Irish Vikings at Brunanburh, possibly Cumbria, in 937 won him the loyalty of all the British rulers, though York (Jorvik) retained its own Viking kings until 954.

Athelstan's court issued a flow of charters and legal documents. The king forged links with foreign rulers through marriage – one of his sisters married the Emperor Otto of Germany; another became wife to Hugh Capet, ruler of the Franks. To cement these alliances, Athelstan was an enthusiastic receiver and giver of jewels, gold and silver, particularly sacred relics.

EDMUND (939–46) AND EADRED (946–55)

Athelstan's brother Edmund the Elder (born *c.* 922) reigned for seven years before meeting an untimely end. During a feast, a gate-crasher named Leof drew a knife and in the resulting struggle Edmund was fatally stabbed. The murderer was 'cut to pieces'. Edmund's brother Eadred had to fight off more troublesome Danes; he was also in constant ill health (the chronicles report he could not eat meat).

EADWIG (955–59) AND EDGAR (959–75)

All the sons of Edward the Elder having reigned in turn, the Crown now passed to the sons of Edmund. Eadwig (Edwy), no more than 13 on becoming king in 955, had a court split by factional conspiracies. The young king – said to be singularly handsome – died before he was 20.

His brother Edgar was just 14 when crowned at Bath, but survived and prospered. Edgar confirmed the English supremacy in Britain, winning allegiance from six Welsh and Scottish kings who are said to have rowed him in state along the River Dee. His reign saw the peak of Saxon achievement in art and scholarship, during which Dunstan of Canterbury, Oswald of York and Ethelwold of Abingdon reformed the monasteries. His court at Winchester was among the most admired in Europe.

'Athelstan king of earls, the lord and rewarder of heroes ...'

The Anglo-Saxon Chronicle *celebrating King Athelstan*

EDWARD THE MARTYR (975–78)

King Edgar died in 975 and was buried at Glastonbury. His son Edward was only 13 and an immediate target for his stepmother Aelfthryth, eager to advance her own son Ethelred. She invited Edward to Corfe, where he was murdered in 978. Edward became a symbol of martyred innocence, elevated to sainthood, but the golden age of the Saxon kings was over.

EDGAR'S CORONATION

The coronation of King Edgar by Dunstan, Archbishop of Canterbury, shown in the Edgar Window at Bath Abbey.

> 'This year [991] was Ipswich ravaged, and after that was Byrhtnoth the Ealdorman slain at Maldon ... and it was decreed that tribute should be given to the Danes, on account of the great terror which they cause.'
>
> The Anglo-Saxon Chronicle

COIN OF ETHELRED

Ethelred proved a weak king, with the knack of picking the wrong people as counsellors. He also had a vicious streak – an unattractive combination.

ETHELRED II UNRAED (978–1016)

ETHELRED'S FIRST NAME COMBINES two Old English words meaning 'noble counsel', but the 'Unraed' either means 'evil advice' or 'treacherous plot', a nickname that may refer to Ethelred gaining the throne through the murder of his half-brother Edward. Later failures merely reinforced his unhappy reputation, so 'Unraed' became 'Unready' – a jibe at the king's inability to defend England against fresh Viking onslaughts. *The Anglo-Saxon Chronicle*, the 'yearbook' of its day, seethes with fury at the incompetence, cowardice and treachery of Ethelred's advisors.

THE BATTLE OF MALDON

In this extract from *The Battle of Maldon*, the leader of the English warriors utters his defiant challenge to the invaders before battle in 991.

'Byrhtnoth gave a speech; he grasped the shield; he brandished the slender ash spear ... here stands a noble earl with his army, who will fight for this country, home of Ethelred my prince, its people and land ... '

Byrhtnoth agreed to let the Vikings leave the tidal island on which they were camped, so the two sides could fight a setpiece battle. The poet emphasizes the importance of the encounter.

'Then was battle near; glory to be grasped.
The time was come when doomed men had to fall.
Uproar was raised there, ravens circled, the eagle craving carrion.
There was tumult on earth.'

Defeat for the English was to prove expensive.

Sensing weakness, the Vikings began a new series of raids, one of which is retold in the heroic poem *The Battle of Maldon* (991). Ethelred reacted by buying off the marauders with money (Danegeld) and grants of land. When this policy failed, the king ordered a massacre in the Danelaw, enraging the Danish king Sweyn. In 1013 a huge Viking army landed, seeking vengeance, and Ethelred fled to Normandy. He came back after Sweyn's death in 1014, only to face renewed invasion from Sweyn's son Cnut (Canute). Ethelred died early in 1016, leaving his son Edmund Ironside to take on Cnut's army.

EDMUND II IRONSIDE (1016)

A firebrand of 22 in 1016, Edmund seems to have despised his ineffectual father. He started a whirlwind campaign against the Danes, and succeeded until the fifth and final battle at Ashingdon, near Rochford in Essex. There the English revival ended with great slaughter – 'all the nobility of the English race was there destroyed' says the *Chronicle* – principally through the treachery of Ethelred's advisor, Eadric, whom Edmund had not removed. The English and Danish kings agreed a truce, but Edmund died shortly afterwards, at Oxford. The way was open for a Dane to rule England.

CNUT AND HIS QUEEN

Cnut's marriage to Emma of Normandy, Ethelred's widow, was a diplomatic union. Here king and queen place a gold cross on the high altar of the New Minster at Winchester.

CNUT (1016–35)

None of Edmund's family could offer a challenge to the Danish king Cnut, who – at the age of 21 – moved onto the vacant throne. People in England wanted leadership and peace, and Cnut proved equal to the job. He removed 'unreliable elements', including not only some worthy nobles but also the treacherous Eadric, who got his just deserts. Taxes were gathered efficiently, the Danish army was paid off, and Cnut took care to show himself to be a pious son of the Church. He also married Ethelred's widow, Emma of Normandy – a shrewd move.

Cnut governed well for 19 years. Ruler of England, Denmark and Norway, and overlord of Scotland, the mighty King Cnut famously rebuked his oily courtiers by demonstrating that the ocean tide was deaf to the commands of even the greatest of kings – or so the story goes.

HARVEST TIME

The Anglo-Saxons were basically farmers, and the agricultural wealth of England made it a tempting prize for foreign adventurers and plunderers – Danes, Norwegians and Normans.

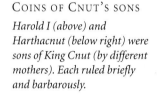

HAROLD I TO EDWARD THE CONFESSOR: 1035–66

HAROLD I (1035–40)

CNUT DIED AT SHAFTESBURY, and was buried at Winchester. 'The illustrious king' of *The Anglo-Saxon Chronicle* had intended his son Harthacnut (whose mother was Queen Emma) to succeed him. But with Harthacnut away in Denmark, his half-brother Harold Harefoot (born in 1017) made himself king at Oxford. Harold I's reign has been described as 'a jackal-time in which packs of scavengers tore at the carcass of Cnut's empire and savaged each other'. Having banished his stepmother and had his half-brother Alfred the Atheling (son of Ethelred) blinded, Harold Harefoot died in 1040 at Oxford, unlamented.

HARTHACNUT (1040–42)

Harthacnut (Hardicanute), a year younger than Harold, was no more likeable. He 'did nothing royal during his whole reign' complained *The Anglo-Saxon Chronicle*, noting that his first act was to demand a large fleet of 72 ships 'at the rate of eight marks for each rower', while the price of wheat rose sharply. The king also had his brother's body exhumed from Westminster and flung into a bog. He treated England as conquered territory, extorted taxes, and died 'in his drink' at a marriage feast where 'he fell to the earth with a terrible convulsion'.

EDWARD THE CONFESSOR (1042–66)

With the Danish line at an end, the House of Wessex returned in the person of Ethelred Unraed's last surviving son. Edward had been born in 1004. Half-Norman, he made no secret of preferring Norman ways and Norman friends. He was chiefly interested in art and religion – hence his devotion to the rebuilding of Westminster Abbey and his descriptive name 'the Confessor'. A man with so little interest in the practicalities of government proved easy prey to politically acute schemers such as Godwin, Earl of Wessex, who unscrupulously moved his own son,

COINS OF CNUT'S SONS
Harold I (above) and Harthacnut (below right) were sons of King Cnut (by different mothers). Each ruled briefly and barbarously.

the soldierly and popular Harold, into position to succeed Edward.

One of Edward's first acts was to seize from his mother Emma 'all the treasures which she possessed ... because before that she had been very hard with the king, her son.' His next move bore the clear mark of Godwin. 'This year Edward took Edgitha, daughter of Earl Godwin, for his wife' says *The Anglo-Saxon Chronicle*.

Edward's reign was largely peaceful, marred by feuding between noble families, and clashes with the Welsh. His chief deficiency was failing to provide an heir; in 1066 his death left a throne hovering between three claimants: Harold of Wessex, William of Normandy and Harald Hardrada of Norway.

A KINGLY BANQUET

This medieval painting shows Edward the Confessor seated at a banquet. Saxon and Norman kings were expected to entertain and reward their followers.

CONFESSOR'S FUNERAL

Edward the Confessor was buried in the church he had built for the purpose. The church was later to become Westminster Abbey.

HAROLD II (1066)

EDWARD'S NORMAN ALLIES had urged him to make Duke William of Normandy his heir, and William was quick to claim the English Crown, with the backing of the Pope in Rome. In England, both the witan (king's noble council) and Church supported Harold of Wessex.

triumphant victory on 25 September at Stamford Bridge, where both Harald and Tostig were killed. On 28 September, a fleet of 700 Norman ships landed at Pevensey on the Sussex coast. Harold wheeled south to face the new threat, without gathering reinforcements.

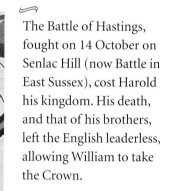

The Battle of Hastings, fought on 14 October on Senlac Hill (now Battle in East Sussex), cost Harold his kingdom. His death, and that of his brothers, left the English leaderless, allowing William to take the Crown.

HAROLD'S MARCHES

This map shows Harold's movements as he tried to counter invasions on two fronts. William by contrast landed, then awaited the battle that would decide his, and England's, destiny.

CONQUEROR AT SEA

Duke William's ship leads the Norman fleet across the Channel. The events of the Conquest are recorded in the Bayeux Tapestry, of which this picture forms part.

Born in 1022, Harold had been supreme in the council since his father Godwin's death in 1053. Named as king by Edward on his deathbed, he was duly crowned. Harold was brave, vigorous and generous. However, while waiting to see what William would do, he was threatened by treachery and invasion. His wayward brother Tostig joined forces with Norway's king Harald Hardrada, and their army landed in the north. Norman historians record that Harold's brother Girth advised him to hold back and that his mother 'hung about him in her great anxiety'. But Harold was no man to hesitate. Marching to Yorkshire, he won a

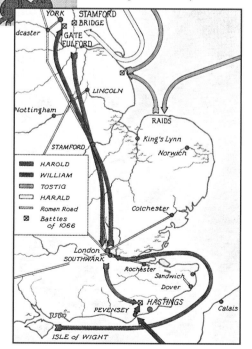

> *'One of the battles which, at rare intervals, have decided the fate of nations.'*
>
> Sir Frank Stenton, historian

History is littered with 'might have beens' and 'what ifs?'. What if Harold had not faced invasion on two fronts in 1066? What if, after Stamford Bridge, he had paused to gather his forces before attacking William?

THE BATTLE OF HASTINGS

At Hastings, the two sides were fairly evenly matched, with estimates of numbers varying from 3,000 to 7,000. The Normans were fresh, however, and their armoured knights on horseback and archers proved decisive. According to Ordericus Vitalis, the Norman monk-historian, the battle was fought 'with the greatest fury' from nine in the morning until the evening. The English wall of shields, axes and spears stood firm under onslaught from arrows and horsemen. At one point William, unhorsed, was feared dead, but he took off his helmet, shouting, **'See, I am here, I am still living and by God's help shall yet have the victory.'** When English troops broke ranks to pursue Normans feigning flight, they were swiftly cut to pieces. By dusk, Harold was dead, along with his brothers Leofwin and Girth, and the hilltop was strewn with bodies. *The Anglo-Saxon Chronicle* comments philosophically **'... the Frenchmen had possession of the place with carnage, all as God granted them for the people's sins'.**

DEATH OF THE LAST SAXON KING
This figure from the Bayeux Tapestry, of an English warrior struck in the eye by an arrow, has often been taken as depicting Harold receiving his death-wound.

Normans and
Plantagenets

WILLIAM I HAD WON a huge gamble, and England was his prize. His followers scooped the rewards, taking over lands from defeated and dispossessed English nobles. William prescribed a government on England that in some ways went further than anything to be found in Normandy. The common people were still able to invoke customary laws, but in great matters such as landholding, taxation and military organization, the Normans imposed their own system.

The Conqueror left three sons to share his legacy. The eldest, Robert, was given Normandy but lost it to a wilier brother. His middle son, William, nicknamed Rufus (from his ruddy complexion), inherited England but then died in mysterious circumstances, leaving the youngest son Henry in possession of the entire family estate. Henry married a descendant of Alfred the Great, a marriage with obvious dynastic overtones, but to his grief lost his only legitimate son in a shipwreck. This left his daughter Matilda to contest the throne with her cousin Stephen, and their tussle brought the Norman dynasty to a rather confused end. On Stephen's death in 1154, the Crown passed to Matilda's son, Henry.

Henry II was first of the Plantagenets, a name inspired by the sprig of broom (*planta genista*) worn by Henry's father, Geoffrey of Anjou. And from Anjou comes the dynasty's alternative name of Angevin. The Plantagenet empire – England, Wales, Ireland, Normandy, Anjou, Brittany and Aquitaine – surpassed any ruled by previous English kings and for the next 300 years kings of England would struggle to keep it.

NORMANS AND PLANTAGENETS

- **William the Conqueror** 1066–1087 = *Matilda of Flanders*
  - *Robert Curthose*
  - **William II** (*Rufus*) 1087–1100
  - **Henry I** 1100–1135 = *Matilda of Scotland*
    - **Matilda** = *Emperor Henry V* (1st husband) = *Geoffrey V Count of Anjou and Maine* (2nd husband)
      - **Henry II** 1154–1189 = *Eleanor of Aquitaine*
        - **Richard I** *Coeur de Lion* 1189–1199
        - **John** 1199–1216 = *Isabella of Angoulême* (2nd wife)
          - **Henry III** 1216–1272 = *Eleanor of Provence*
            - **Edward I** 1272–1307 = *Eleanor of Castile*
              - **Edward II** 1307–1327 = *Isabella of France*
                - **Edward III** 1327–1377 = *Philippa of Hainault*
          - *Joan* = **Alexander II** *King of Scotland*
          - *Eleanor* = *Simon de Montfort* (2nd husband)
  - *Adela* = *Stephen Count of Blois*
    - **Stephen** 1135–1154

Descendants of Edward III:
- *Edward the Black Prince* = *Joan of Kent*
  - **Richard II** 1377–1399
- *Lionel* = *Elizabeth de Burgh*
  - *Philippa* = *Edmund Mortimer*
    - *Roger Mortimer* = *Eleanor Holland*
    - **HOUSE OF YORK**
      - *Anne Mortimer* = *Richard Earl of Cambridge*
        - *Richard Duke of York* = *Cecily Neville*
          - **Edward IV** 1461–1470 restored 1471–1483 = *Elizabeth Woodville*
            - **Edward V** April–June 1483 *Princes in the Tower*
            - *Richard Duke of York* *Princes in the Tower*
            - *Elizabeth of York* = **Henry VII** 1485–1509 (*Henry Tudor*)
          - *George Duke of Clarence*
          - **Richard III** 1483–1485 = *Anne daughter of Richard Neville (Kingmaker)* = *Edward Prince of Wales* (1st husband)
            - *Edward Prince of Wales*
- *Joan* = **David II** *King of Scotland*
- **John of Gaunt** = *Blanche of Lancaster* (1st wife)
  - **HOUSE OF LANCASTER**
    - **Henry IV** 1399–1413 = *Mary de Bohun*
      - **Henry V** 1413–1422 = *Catherine of France*
        - **Henry VI** 1422–1461 restored 1470–1471 = *Margaret of Anjou*

HOUSES OF BEAUFORT AND TUDOR
See page 51

21

WILLIAM I (1066–87)

BORN IN 1028, WILLIAM was the elder of two illegitimate sons born to Arlette of Falaise and Duke Robert I of Normandy (d. 1035). He grew up in a murderous atmosphere, protected by his determined mother, but by the age of 15 was strong enough to begin his own rule. William soon proved a vigorous soldier, defeating rebels to enforce his rule on Normandy; his methods were simple, often brutal, always effective. But William was more than a Viking throwback, impressing others by his fierce will, physical strength, love of hunting, and disciplined habits. He was a faithful husband to his wife Matilda, who bore at least nine children and acted as regent in Normandy while William was away conquering England.

William's interest in England seems to have begun in his teens, when he met Edward the Confessor during Edward's exile in France. A promise of the Crown may have been made in 1051, and in 1064/65 – according to Norman sources – William also extracted a forced promise from Harold Godwinson that the throne of England would pass to William when Edward died.

As soon as Harold was declared king in January 1066, William began war preparations. He crossed the Channel unopposed, landed his force successfully, established a bridgehead with prefabricated forts, and met the English in battle at Hastings on 14 October. This was a feat of military genius, and William's brave leadership on that fateful day

THE DOMESDAY BOOK

William made only four visits to England between 1072 and 1087. The last occasion was noteworthy for the most astonishing feat of Norman bureaucracy – William's survey of the kingdom, known as the Domesday Book. Nothing like it had been attempted before. County by county, landholdings were listed, described and assessed for tax and value, with comparisons drawn between 1066 and 1086. For historians, the Domesday Book is a price-less record, giving a fascinating 'snapshot' in civil servants' language of the land the Normans found.

'St Peter's of Westminster holds Patricesy [Battersea]. Earl Harold held it [in 1066]. Then it answered for 72 hides, now for 18 hides ... 45 villagers and 16 smallholders with 14 ploughs. 8 slaves, 7 mills ... woodland at 50 pigs ...'

Battersea: from the Domesday Book

CASTLES ACROSS THE LAND

The Normans embarked on a programme of castle-building, in which William (like most medieval kings) took a keen personal interest. Notice the workmen's hod and trowel, unchanged today.

secured the Normans' victory and his title of Conqueror. English resistance flickered for some years, but William put down all rebellions with relentless severity. The old Saxon nobility lost their lands to Norman knights, and a similar Normanization took place in the Church. Unlike Cnut, who ruled England as he found it, William the Conqueror stamped his seal on England and reshaped it. The Domesday Book was an expression of the new system, and a testament to the ruler who caused it to be made. When William I died in 1087, Norman rule was secure.

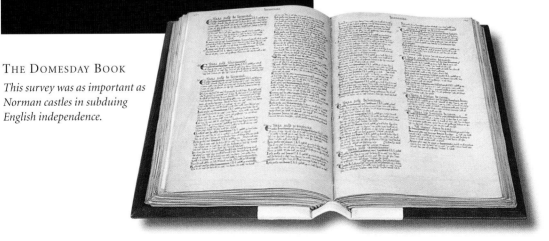

THE DOMESDAY BOOK

This survey was as important as Norman castles in subduing English independence.

23

THE NORMANS' CASTLES

The White Tower, which dominates the Tower of London, is England's largest and oldest keep. It stands 27 metres (90 feet) high and its walls are 4.6 metres (15 feet) thick at the base.

WINDSOR CASTLE IN THE 11TH CENTURY

This modern painting shows Windsor Castle as it looked when newly built by the Normans in 1080. There are two separate baileys, with the motte or mound in the middle, and a wooden tower on top.

ALTHOUGH WILLIAM MAY NOT have been wanted by the English, they had little choice but to put up with him. He treated the country as dangerous occupied territory, subdued and held by a chain of forts. A line of castles soon stretched from Warwick to York, dominating the Midlands, with another in eastern England passing through Lincoln, Huntingdon and Cambridge. English resistance in the north and east received Danish support, as Sweyn Esthrithsson of Denmark nursed ambitions for a still shaky throne. William's counterstrokes were savage. The north was 'harried'; peasants were slaughtered, crops burned, tools and ploughs destroyed. Monasteries too were plundered. The Conqueror's castles dominated the countryside, a stark reminder of William's brooding power.

Norman castles were of the 'motte and bailey' type. An area of land (the bailey) was surrounded by a ditch and bank, topped by a palisade. Within the bailey, or beside it, was a steep-sided mound (the motte), on top of which stood a wooden tower or donjon, the residence of the castle owner. Such castles could be built in about a week, using forced labour. From such a stronghold, a small group of men could control the surrounding country.

CLERICAL ABSEILER MAKES DARING GETAWAY

Under William II's brother, Henry I, the Tower gained a new use – as a prison. The first dignitary to be locked up there was Ranulf Flambard, Bishop of Durham, arrested by Henry in 1100. Unlike most of the unfortunates who were to follow him, Ranulf made a successful escape with the help of a smuggled-in rope.

About 200 castles were built in the 35 years following the Norman Conquest. Early wooden buildings were soon replaced by massive castles of stone, among them the Tower of London, for under the Normans London became the undisputed capital of England. Foundations for the White Tower, stronghold of the Tower of London, were laid about 1078 under the direction of Gundulf, a monk from Normandy who later became Bishop of Rochester. Still unfinished when William I died in 1087, it was completed about 1097 by William II.

A COASTAL GUARDIAN

Henry II built the square keep of Dover Castle, guarding the sea approach to southern England. Begun in 1181 and completed in 1189, Dover's was among the last of the great square keeps.

'The Normans, when under the rule of a kind but firm master, are a most valiant people.'

Ordericus Vitalis, Norman historian

NORMANS ANNOY DOVER

Dover was an early target for the Normans after Hastings. According to William of Poitiers' account of the Norman Conquest, '[Dover was] situated on a rock adjoining the sea … **it stands like a straight wall as high as an arrow's flight.** Our men, greedy for booty, set fire to the castle while the inhabitants were preparing to surrender'. William offered compensation – then set about rebuilding the walls.

WILLIAM II TO STEPHEN: 1087–1154

WILLIAM II (1087–1100)

HIS STRENGTH AND GIRTH marked William Rufus as a son of the Conqueror. Born in 1056, he was reckless, greedy and opportunistic – qualities which won approval from his knights, but earned the displeasure of monks who condemned with distaste the fashions of his court – long hair, pointed shoes and effeminate behaviour. William II had himself crowned soon after his father's death, and continued the Conqueror's task of crushing rebellion among the English while extending Norman rule into South Wales and northern England.

A HUNTING ACCIDENT?

The death of William II seems to have been accepted as an accident. The man blamed for the fatal bowshot, Walter Tirel, fled abroad, but his family received favours from Henry I – was this coincidence?

William I had turned great tracts of land into hunting parks, and his sons were equally enthusiastic huntsmen. In August 1100, William Rufus was killed in the New Forest, apparently by a stray arrow. The king's brother Henry, also hunting that day, rushed to Winchester to lay his hands on the royal treasury. Rufus's body was carted off for unroyal burial beneath the cathedral tower and – three days after his brother's death – Henry I was crowned King of England.

WESTMINSTER HALL

Westminster Hall was built by William Rufus between 1097–99, alongside the palace constructed for Edward the Confessor and used as a residence by William the Conqueror.

' … he was well built, his complexion florid, his hair yellow … of astonishing strength though not very tall and his belly rather projecting … '

William of Malmesbury (d. c. 1143) on William Rufus

HENRY I (1100–35)

'Of middle stature, his hair black, his chest brawny', Henry was, according to William of Malmesbury, 'the master of his passions, rather than their slave'. William also comments that 'his sleep was heavy and marked by much snoring'.

Henry had all the Norman ruthlessness. False-coiners (counterfeiters) in England were mutilated on his orders to discourage others from following their example. In 1106 he defeated his brother Robert, locked him up, and thereafter sat easy on the English throne. Henry's diplomatic triumph was to marry his daughter Matilda to the Holy Roman Emperor in 1114, but in 1120 the loss of his son William, drowned in the Channel, was a personal and dynastic disaster.

Henry fixed his ambitions on the Empress Matilda, now a widow, making his barons swear allegiance to her, and 'her lawful husband, should she have one'. Matilda married again; she and Geoffrey, Count of Anjou, were ill-matched but produced two sons: Henry, in 1133, and Geoffrey a year later.

STEPHEN (1135–54) AND MATILDA

'A man of activity but imprudent', Stephen of Blois was the nephew of Henry I. He had charm, geniality, dash and personal bravery. Enough barons liked him, despite his inability to sustain any action, to back him for the kingship in 1135 when Henry I died. Stephen was at once challenged by his cousin Matilda, and a patchily vicious civil war ensued, with anarchy at its worst between 1139 and 1145. Neither side could land the killer blow. Both cousins had sons, but when Stephen's son Eustace died before his father, all parties agreed that Matilda's son, Henry, must be the next king. Matilda had won the final family battle.

HENRY II TO RICHARD I: 1154–99

HENRY II (1154–89)

'ONE OF THE MOST remarkable characters in English history', Henry II (born 1133) ruled an empire larger than any English king before him. It included England, Wales, Ireland, Anjou, Normandy, Brittany and Aquitaine. His prestige rivalled that of the Holy Roman Emperor Frederick Barbarossa, while Henry's wife, Eleanor of Aquitaine – one of the most formidable and dynamic women of medieval times – matched him in power of will.

Henry was 'medieval action man'; robust, physically impressive, and restlessly active in war, the hunt, the law, letters, art and architecture. His rages struck onlookers with terror; his charm bewitched them. Henry's iron will awed his subjects and imposed his policies on his country. His most lasting achievement was reconstruction of the English legal system.

Yet it was Henry's quarrels, rather than his law-making, that most impressed at the time and his most infamous dispute – with his friend and chancellor, Thomas Becket – echoed through the centuries. This was both a clash of wills and a conflict between rights of Church and Crown. Its result was Becket's murder in Canterbury Cathedral in 1170. Whether or not Henry knowingly commanded the murder is debatable, but he did public penance for it. His later quarrels with Queen Eleanor and his sons provoked a vicious civil war that threatened to dismember the empire.

WHERE A KING DID PENANCE

Henry II, pictured in stained glass in the Trinity Chapel of Canterbury Cathedral. In a public show of remorse and guilt for Becket's death, the king was scourged (beaten) by monks the following year. Becket's shrine became a place of pilgrimage, and the chapel's Miracle Window shows scenes of miracles attributed to the saint.

THE ENGLISH POPE

Nicholas Breakspear became Pope in 1154, taking the name of Adrian IV. At his death in 1159, the only English Pope was 'lamented by all good men'. One of his acts was to grant 'the illustrious king of England', Henry II, hereditary possession of Ireland.

RICHARD'S CORONATION

Richard's coronation procession approaches Westminster. England was a peripheral interest throughout the reign of this soldier king who also wrote poetry.

A CRUSADER

This 12th-century drawing of a crusader shows his calf-length hauberk (coat of mail) and lance. The First Crusade of 1096 was followed by a further seven expeditions of Europeans to the Holy Land.

SETTING SAIL FOR THE EAST

Richard of Devizes describes how Richard I assembled a fleet of over 100 ships for his crusade in 1190. The biggest, known as busses, had 30 oars and two sails and carried 40 horses **'well trained for war'** along with knights and foot-soldiers, and a year's stores. The 'exceedingly great' royal treasure was split between the ships, for safety.

RICHARD I (COEUR DE LION) (1189–99)

It has been said of Richard that 'few English kings have played so small a part in the affairs of England'. Born in 1157 at Oxford, Richard was the second surviving son of Henry II and Queen Eleanor. He grew up in France where he learned soldiering by fighting the barons of Aquitaine. An admired if reckless soldier and crusader alongside his friend King Philip of France, Richard spent less than five months of his reign in England. For some Englishmen, this made him an ideal monarch.

Richard fought in France, Sicily and in Palestine during the Third Crusade, earning the respect of the Muslim leader Saladin but failing to recapture Jerusalem. His military career, though impressive, was expensive and culminated in a huge ransom bill when – in 1192 – the home-bound king was held hostage by Leopold of Austria. Managing such affairs was left to the capable Hubert Walter, Archbishop of Canterbury. Richard's marriage to Berengaria of Navarre produced no children (the king may well have been homosexual) and in 1192 carelessness during a minor siege resulted in a crossbow wound that cost him his life at the age of 42. The Lionheart passed into legend, and his brother John became king.

JOHN AND HENRY III: 1199–1272

'He was a great prince but hardly a happy one.'

Annals of Barnwell Priory, on King John

JOHN (1199–1216)

JOHN, BORN 1167, was nicknamed 'Lackland' by his father Henry II, though he gained large estates through gifts and marriage to Isabella of Gloucester. Capable, clever, scheming and untrustworthy, John conspired against both his father and brother, trying to seize the throne in 1193 during Richard's absence. On becoming king in 1199, he struggled to prevent Henry's empire from fragmenting, but died in 1216 in the shadow of failure, his name forever linked to Magna Carta – called the 'greatest constitutional document of all times' – signed by the Thames at Runnymede.

In 1204, John lost control of Normandy, a humiliation that earned him the mocking name 'soft-sword'. 'No man may ever trust him, for his heart is soft and cowardly,' sang the troubadour Bertrand de Born. To maintain his grip on England and win back lost lands in France, John rode roughshod over the rights of Church and nobles. He also raised taxes – stirring up more unrest.

THE KING GOES A'HUNTING

All medieval kings enjoyed hunting and hawking, and John was no exception. He was also literate and good at the details of government.

JOHN'S TOMB

King John died of dysentery at Newark in 1216. His tomb is situated in the chancel of Worcester Cathedral.

MAGNA CARTA

Magna Carta is a major landmark in constitutional history, but also a backward look at the failings of previous reigns. Though later generations saw it as 'the corner-stone of English liberties', the fact that the king was forced to make concessions was more important than the concessions themselves. King John saw the charter as a strategy to buy time. He had no intention of surrendering kingly rights, but in 1297 Magna Carta became law. Nine of its chapters are still on the statute book. Even more important was its symbolic status; in America it played a part in shaping the 1776 Declaration of Independence.

*'At Runnymede,
at Runnymede,
Your rights were won
at Runnymede!'*

Rudyard Kipling

In 1215 a rebellious group of nobles backed John into a corner, forcing him to agree to the 'rights' enshrined in Magna Carta. John was still fighting the French (having, by tradition, added loss of the crown jewels in the Wash to that of Normandy) when he died in 1216.

HENRY III (1216–72)

Born at Winchester in 1207, Henry was the eldest son of King John and his second wife, Isabella of Angoulême. Still a minor, Henry began his reign under a regent, William Marshal, Earl of Pembroke. From 1234 Henry took government into his own hands, and in 1236 married Eleanor of Provence, proving a faithful husband and tolerant father. Described by the chronicler Nicholas Trivet as 'of moderate stature, with the lid of one eye rather drooping, robust in strength but impulsive in action', he flew into rages whenever challenged and his choice of toadying foreign councillors offended the English nobility.

In 1258, Henry grudgingly accepted a baronial 'Privy Council'. The following year he signed away more lands to the French king, Louis IX, so that now only Gascony remained in English hands. Henry's brother-in-law, Simon de Montfort, was the sharpest thorn in the king's flesh. Clever and popular, in 1263 de Montfort led a revolt and at Lewes (12 May 1264) captured Prince Edward (later Edward I). He then summoned a parliament – of barons, knights from the shires and burgesses from the towns – seen as the forerunner of modern parliaments. In 1265, however, Prince Edward turned the tables at Evesham, where de Montfort was killed. The last six years of Henry's reign passed peacefully.

LESS TALENTED THAN HE THOUGHT
Henry III's tomb-effigy in Westminster Abbey. Henry had a somewhat exalted view of his royal status, but lacked real royal ability.

EDWARD I AND EDWARD II: 1272–1327

EDWARD I (1272–1307)

'THE PATTERN OF THE medieval king', Edward was born in 1239. Eldest son of Henry III, he married Eleanor of Castile in 1254. His headstrong nature led to a temporary split with his father during the de Montfort rebellion, and it was on his way back from Palestine in 1272 that Edward learned of Henry's death.

Tall and handsome, Edward was happiest on horseback with hunting dogs at his heels and a hawk on his wrist, or when making war on the Welsh and Scots. In 1284 Wales was formally annexed to the English Crown and the king built a chain of castles around the Welsh, to choke resistance.

When King Alexander III of Scotland died in 1286, Edward decided to assert his overlordship of the Scots. First he planned to marry Alexander's granddaughter Margaret ('The Maid of Norway') to his son, but Margaret died in 1290. Claimants to the vacant Scots throne were then submitted to Edward, who provoked the Scottish lords when he chose John Balliol. Edward led an English army north, defeating the Scots at Falkirk in 1298. Forced to renew hostilities in 1303, he captured the Scots' leader William Wallace, who suffered a traitor's gruesome death in 1305. Following Wallace came a new Scots hero, Robert the Bruce, crowned in 1306. On his way north to yet another battle, Edward I – the 'hammer of the Scots' – died near Carlisle on 7 July 1307.

EDWARD II (1307–27)

Although handsome, like his father Edward I, Edward II was less astute and more eccentric – his interest in ditch-digging, for instance, raised eyebrows at court. So did his affection for Piers Gaveston, a Gascon knight. Edward's marriage in 1308 to Isabella, daughter of King Philip IV of France, produced a son (the future Edward III) but Gaveston's closeness to the king aroused such resentment that in 1312 rebel barons killed him. The king burned for revenge.

MONARCH OVER ALL

An imaginary scene of Edward I in Parliament, flanked by King Alexander III of Scotland and the last prince to rule Wales, Llywelyn ap Gruffydd.

Instead, he suffered further humiliation, in Scotland, where in 1314 Robert the Bruce crushed the English army.

Edward inflamed the situation by appointing Hugh le Despenser and his son to run the country. The barons revolted; the Despensers were sacked, then reinstated; leading rebels were executed. It was a familiar pattern, made worse by French meddling: the king of France seized Edward's French lands. Queen Isabella (thoroughly weary of her husband) took as her lover a leading baron-in-exile, Roger Mortimer, and the pair arrived in England from France in 1326. The Despensers were put to death as traitors. Edward was jailed at Kenilworth, ruled incompetent to govern, then moved to Berkeley Castle in Gloucestershire where he was almost certainly murdered (allegedly with a red-hot iron).

CASTLES OF WALES

To secure his conquest of Wales, Edward I built castles to dominate key routes, on sites where they could be supplied by sea. His great castles (Beaumaris, Caernarfon, Caerphilly, Conwy, Flint and Harlech) represent the peak of medieval military architecture in Britain. Directing a vast army of workers was Master James of St George, a master-builder from Savoy (France).

EDWARD III (1327–77)

'The English will never love and honour a king unless he be victorious and a lover of arms and war.' Froissart, French chronicler

THE BATTLE OF CRÉCY

Crécy, won in 1346. It was one of the most crushing English victories in France, and the first battle in which English troops used crude cannon.

BORN IN 1312, EDWARD was under 15 when crowned in January 1327, and at first had to submit to the regency of his mother Isabella and her lover Roger Mortimer. In 1330, however, he had Mortimer executed and sent his mother into retirement. England was now his. To distract his squabbling nobles, he set about the country's traditional foreign enemies: France and Scotland.

WITNESSES TO DEVASTATION

An Oxfordshire cleric, Geoffrey le Baker, described the horrors of the Black Death: **'As the graveyards did not suffice, fields were chosen for the burial of the dead … it was the young and strong that the plague chiefly attacked.'**

The effect on the economy was drastic: 'The following autumn no one could get a reaper for less than 8d with his food, a mower for less than 12d with his food … wherefore many crops perished in the fields …' wrote Henry Knighton, a monk of Leicester.

EDWARD AND SON
Edward III, shown in this picture with his son, the Black Prince. They were the most famous royal soldiers in Europe.

Robert the Bruce's death in 1329 gave Edward the chance to oust the young Scots King David II and install a puppet ruler – John Balliol's son Edward. In 1340 England's king also proclaimed himself King of France, and so began the Hundred Years' War. An active commander, Edward was on board ship during the naval victory at Sluys in 1340. In 1346, the king and his son Edward (the Black Prince) won the Battle of Crécy, and established Calais as an English colony. The king of Scotland was captured at the Battle of Neville's Cross (1346), as was the king of France at the later Battle of Poitiers (1356). In 1348, Edward turned down the chance to be Holy Roman Emperor: it was the high point of his reign.

Then in 1348–49 the Black Death struck, killing about one-third of England's population, and after 1360 the tide of war in France turned against Edward. His queen, Philippa of Hainault, died in 1369 and his eldest son, Edward the Black Prince, returned from the wars in 1371 broken in health. The next year King Edward made one last foray across the Channel, but adverse winds kept him from landing on French soil. In 1375 he was glad to make peace, relapsing into senility under the thumb of his greedy mistress, Alice Perrers.

The two most prominent of his twelve children, the Black Prince and John of Gaunt, were at loggerheads, and the Prince's death in 1376 left Gaunt in overall command. Gaunt and his brother Edmund Langley bequeathed a significant legacy to history as founders of the houses of Lancaster and York, later contestants in the Wars of the Roses. But when Edward III – once Europe's most famous knight – died at Sheen in 1377, his grandson Richard of Bordeaux walked uncertainly towards his throne.

THE GARTER KNIGHTS

The Order of the Garter, England's most famous order of knighthood, was founded by Edward III in 1348 – in part inspired by his desire to recreate the aura of King Arthur's Round Table Knights. Its emblem is a blue garter edged with gold, worn below the left knee. Tradition holds that the king gallantly picked up the garter of a court lady during a dance with the remark, *'Honi soit qui mal y pense'* ('Shame be to him who thinks evil of it'). The reigning monarch is Sovereign of the Order.

BANNERS OF THE GARTER KNIGHTS
Banners of the Knights of the Garter hang in St George's Chapel, at Windsor Castle.

RICHARD II AND HENRY IV: 1377–1413

THE KING IN COURT

Richard II holding court after his coronation. Cynicism, corruption and perfidy seem to have surrounded the young king.

RICHARD THE KING

This painting of Richard II is the earliest portrait of a reigning English king. Talented and inventive, he made a brave beginning at Smithfield.

RICHARD II (1377–99)

BORN IN THE FRENCH city of Bordeaux in 1367, Richard was the youngest son of Edward the Black Prince and Joan of Kent. The Black Prince died in 1376, and a year later the death of Edward III left his ten-year-old grandson as England's king.

Richard's first public act was courageous. In 1381 he rode out from London to confront a rebel army at Smithfield during the Peasants' Revolt. The peasant leader Wat Tyler – wounded by London's mayor, William Walworth – was later beheaded. Peace was restored but the Speaker of the House of Commons voiced a general fear of rule by a boy-king: 'The whole kingdom will be lost and utterly destroyed forever, and the King and Lords and Commons with it'.

In 1382, Richard married Anne of Bohemia (who died in 1394). Artistic and sensitive, he was patron of the writers Chaucer and Gower and oversaw the rebuilding of Westminster Hall. But militarily he was inept, and disastrously alienated his powerful uncle, John of Gaunt, Duke of Lancaster. Factional infighting pushed Richard to declare that he would rule alone, without the aid of quarrelsome elders. In 1396 he married Isabella of France, and then turned on his noble enemies, banishing among them his cousin Henry Bolingbroke, John of Gaunt's son. In 1399 the king recklessly moved to seize the Gaunt estates, playing into the hands of ambitious Bolingbroke, who invaded England to seize the Crown while Richard was in Ireland.

Richard fell helplessly into the trap. He surrendered the throne and was imprisoned at Pontefract Castle. There he died in February 1400, possibly murdered, but more likely starved to death.

HENRY IV (1399–1413)

Henry IV was born in 1367 at Bolingbroke Castle in Lincolnshire, the son of John of Gaunt and Blanche of Lancaster. With a debatable claim to the throne, Henry's grasp on the Crown was fragile and until 1405 his reign was plagued by uprisings in Wales, led by Owen Glyndwr, and in the north. The king was ill, fearful of assassination and troubled by a guilty conscience.

Despite these problems, Henry IV was successful. He survived to pass on England's Crown to his heir, whose youthful misdemeanours had taxed his patience. Though Henry's death caused little grief, and his reign lacked ambition or achievement, his son was to write a very different story in the annals of English history.

'Uneasy lies the head that wears a crown …'

Henry IV Part II, *William Shakespeare*

RICHARD'S CAPTURE

A French manuscript illustrates the arrest of Richard II in 1399 at Flint Castle. His captor, Bolingbroke, proclaimed himself king.

HENRY IV IN FUNEREAL GRANDEUR

Henry IV's effigy on his Canterbury Cathedral tomb suggests a rather stately regality, not the dashing power-hunter that was the youthful Bolingbroke.

THE COOL COMMANDER

Henry V could be cold and ruthless, yet he inspired devotion among his followers, 'the band of brothers' as Shakespeare later called them.

VICTORY AT AGINCOURT

This was Henry's most remarkable victory. His army of some 5,000 men defeated a French force perhaps four times larger, with minimal casualties (said to be around 100 compared to the French losses of over 5,000).

'The most serene prince ... he was very well-favoured ... he outstripped all his equals in age at running and jumping ...'

Life of Henry V,
Thomas de Elmham

HENRY V (1413–22)

HENRY WAS BORN AT MONMOUTH in 1387. His father was Henry Bolingbroke; his mother, Mary de Bohun, daughter of the Earl of Hereford. During the period that Bolingbroke was in exile (October 1398–July 1399), the young Henry stayed with his father's cousin Richard II, and was knighted by him in Ireland.

Henry was intelligent and musical, reading and writing English (perhaps the first post-Norman king to do so with ease). From 1402 he commanded his father's army against the Welsh. Stories of his dissolute youth, later dramatized by Shakespeare, probably have some basis in fact since the stories began within 20 years of Henry's death.

Henry V became king on 21 March 1413, almost at once turning his attention to France, not just to reassert old claims but also to eye lands never before held by an English king. To boundless ambition, the young king added martial vigour, piety, a commanding character, and a streak of ruthlessness – qualities that elevated his nine-year reign to epic status. He led two great expeditions to France (1415 and 1417–18). At Agincourt in October 1415, English archers mowed down the French knights in swathes. Henry seemed invincible.

The Treaty of Troyes in 1420 recognized Henry as heir to the French throne. He married Catherine of Valois, daughter of the French king Charles VI, and dreamed of a new crusade to Palestine. But triumph was short-lived. In 1422 the king contracted dysentery, dying in August at Bois de Vincennes. His body was taken home for burial in Westminster Abbey. Henry was not to have France, and his premature death plunged England once more into dynastic wars.

*'Was ever king that joy'd an earthly throne
And could command no more content than I?'*

Henry, in William Shakespeare's King Henry VI Part II

HENRY VI (1422–61) AND (1470–71)

A new age of uncertainties was dawning as Henry V's baby son, Henry VI, stayed under the 'care and control' of his relatives until 1437. After an English coronation in 1429, in 1431 young Henry was crowned king of France. But across the Channel events were turning against England.

Religious and studious, reclusive Henry had no taste for war. Some thought him simple-minded, for he suffered bouts of nervous collapse that were called 'madness'. He founded Eton College and King's College, Cambridge, but lost all his father's conquests in France, where the French rallied under the inspirational Joan of Arc. At home, Jack Cade's rebellion (1450) showed serious weakness in the realm.

Richard, Duke of York, was made Lord Protector in 1454, but his hopes of seizing the Crown were dashed by the king's recovery to health – and the birth of Henry's son Edward in 1453. York's chance lay in civil war, which began in 1455.

Henry, a helpless pawn in these 'Wars of the Roses', was captured (1460), rescued (1461), deposed, recaptured (1465), imprisoned, reinstated (1470) and then murdered (1471). Despised and mocked in life, Henry was popularly venerated as a saint after his death.

SCHOLARLY KING

A bronze statuette of Henry VI, from the lectern of King's College Chapel, Cambridge. Henry's educational foundations, including Eton College, were inspired by his admiration for the work of William of Wykeham a century earlier.

WARS OF THE ROSES

'The Queen Margaret is verily landed and her son in the west country, and I trow that as tomorrow, or else the next day, King Edward will depart from hence to her ward to drive her out again.' Extract from one of the Paston Letters, written after the Battle of Barnet, 1471

THE WARS OF THE ROSES were ferocious struggles for power, with England as the prize. The warring parties were the House of Lancaster (whose symbol was a red rose) and the House of York (a white rose). Both families claimed Edward III as their royal ancestor, and so both laid hands on the Crown.

The soldier-hero Henry V had died too soon, leaving a child-king – Henry VI. This boy grew up to be an incompetent

A KING CAPTURED

Henry VI was captured after the Battle of Northampton which took place on 10 July 1460. A respectful Earl of Warwick (a Yorkist ally at this stage) kneels before the unfortunate king.

KEY BATTLES OF THE WARS OF THE ROSES

St Albans 22 May 1455	Yorkist victory
Northampton 10 July 1460	Yorkist victory: Henry VI captured
Wakefield 21 December 1460	Lancastrian victory: York killed
St Albans 17 February 1461	Lancastrian victory
Towton 29 March 1461	Yorkist victory: Edward IV becomes king
Barnet 14 April 1471	Yorkist victory: Warwick killed
Tewkesbury 4 May 1471	Yorkist victory: Prince Edward killed
Bosworth 22 August 1485	Lancastrian/Tudor victory: Richard III is killed and Henry VII becomes king

bookworm, ruled by a domineering queen, Margaret, who made many enemies. France was lost, the nation's coffers were empty, the nobility disgruntled. When Henry collapsed into mental illness in 1453, the Duke of York decided enough was enough, and set about making a bid for the throne.

The iron-willed Queen Margaret stiffened Lancastrian resistance, dashing York's hopes for an easy transfer to power. The grand old duke's ambition ended in defeat and shame – his severed head, crowned with paper, stuck on a pole above the gates of York. But the duke had capable sons: Edward (later Edward IV) and Richard (later Richard III). Faced with such military muscle, the Lancastrians wobbled. King Henry was powerless whether in the hands of friends or foes, leaving Lancastrian hopes with Queen Margaret, her son (the young Prince Edward) and the fickle Earl of Warwick, 'the Kingmaker'.

Having helped Edward to the throne after the Battle of Towton (1461), Warwick later changed sides. Henry was briefly restored as king in 1470, but the pendulum quickly swung back to the Yorkists. Warwick was killed at Barnet, and Prince Edward at Tewkesbury – a cruel blow to Queen Margaret. When Henry VI followed his son to the grave, Edward IV seemed secure, but his death in 1483 opened an opportunity for his brother Richard. The disappearance of the Princes in the Tower and one last

IRON QUEEN

Margaret of Anjou married Henry VI in 1445 at the age of 16. Beautiful, clever and forceful, her iron will kept the Lancastrians in the field through disaster and defeat.

bloody battle – Bosworth in 1485 – were the final twists in the violent chronicles of the Wars of the Roses. Henry Tudor's victory at Bosworth began a fresh chapter of English regal history.

41

EDWARD IV (1461–70) AND (1471–83)

BORN IN 1442, EDWARD was the son of Richard, Duke of York, and Cicely Neville. Four years later, York made his bid for the throne and so kindled the Wars of the Roses. After the duke's death in 1460, his youthful, handsome son Edward became the Yorkist claimant, backed by his cousin Richard Neville, Earl of Warwick, 'the Kingmaker'. Victory at Towton in 1461 deposed Henry VI and gave Edward the Crown.

Tall and engaging, Edward was also un-reliable, self-indulgent and a womanizer. A Frenchman, Philippe de Commynes, commented that Edward 'thought upon nothing but women'. But his dashing skill on the battlefield was undeniable. Dissent between the Yorkist cousins arose after Edward secretly married Elizabeth Woodville in 1464 – money and promises having failed to gain her favours. This union wrecked Warwick's plan for a royal marriage with a French princess (a deal for which the French king was willing to reward Warwick handsomely). Moreover, the new queen had power-hungry relatives, whose fortunes she was eager to advance. Warwick was sidelined, especially when the king made it clear he favoured Burgundy, rather than France, as an ally.

Between 1469 and 1471, a serious crisis faced the Yorkists when Warwick switched

TEWKESBURY SLAUGHTER

The Battle of Tewkesbury, in May 1471, was among the bloodiest of Roses conflicts. The name 'Bloody Meadow' survives from the day that effectively secured the Crown for Edward IV.

A KING BESET BY HIS IN-LAWS

Edward is shown in this paint-ing with Elizabeth Woodville and their young son, Edward V. Woodville relatives cluster greedily around the fount of wealth and influence.

to the Lancastrian side, causing Edward to flee to Burgundy in 1470. Warwick put Henry VI back on the throne, but in March 1471 Edward came home with Burgundian troops to boost his cause. Battlefield victories at Barnet (where Warwick was killed) and Tewkesbury (where Henry VI's son Prince Edward died) restored Edward IV to power. Henry was put to death and the king reigned securely.

Edward ruled well for his last 12 years, though the execution for treason of his brother Clarence (traditionally drowned in a wine butt) and the influence of the Woodville clan alarmed and incensed other nobles. A lover of books, who found the new printing press fascinating, the king grew fat and lazy, relaxing in the company of his mistress Jane Shore. When Edward died suddenly in 1483, he left two sons – neither of them old enough to grasp the Crown securely. Beside them – as he had stood by Edward through the bloody civil wars – hovered the brooding figure of the king's brother, Richard, Duke of Gloucester.

'This Edward was a goodly man … of stature high, of countenance and beauty comely … of a pregnant wit … and high of courage … '

Extract from the Chronicle of John Hardyng (1378–1464)

PENSIVE POWER-SEEKER

Edward IV inherited the dynastic ambitions of his father, Richard of York, claiming to be true heir to the deposed Richard II.

WARWICK: CASTLE FOR A KINGMAKER

WARWICK CASTLE

Warwick Castle, once home of the Kingmaker, now houses a modern exhibition portraying the Wars of the Roses.

THOUGH NEVER CALLED 'KINGMAKER' in his lifetime, Richard Neville, Earl of Warwick (1428–71) was, during the Wars of the Roses, the most important power-broker in England. A great-great-grandson of Edward III (and potential claimant to the throne), he gained vast wealth by marrying Anne Beauchamp, the richest heiress of the age.

The Nevilles had supported the Yorkist side since 1453 and, after his father's death, Warwick helped Edward IV to the throne in 1461. But his friendship with Edward soured after the king married Elizabeth Woodville. Fretting at being sidelined by the Woodville clan, he skilfully secured French support and engineered a revolt (1469–70) that briefly won back the throne for the deposed Henry VI. Edward proved resilient, however, and a better general.

The two former allies clashed at Barnet in 1471 where Warwick (fighting on foot to stiffen his troops' resolve) was cut off and killed during the Lancastrian rout. His daughter Anne married Edward's brother Richard of Gloucester (later Richard III) the following year.

Able, rich and politically ingenious, Warwick was both admired and feared. Only inferiority as a battlefield commander undermined him in the tangled struggles of the Wars of the Roses. Had victory at Barnet gone to Lancaster and not York, Warwick would have been lauded at Henry VI's side – or perhaps taken the Crown himself.

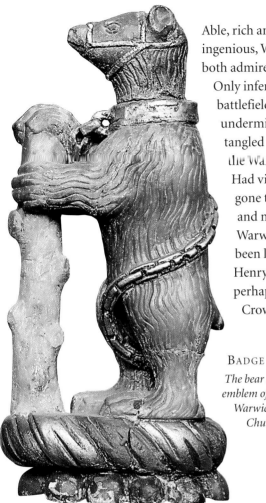

BADGE OF WARWICK

The bear and ragged staff, emblem of the earls of Warwick; in St Mary's Church, Warwick.

In this painting of the Battle of Barnet, 14 April 1471, Edward IV is shown symbolically besting Warwick, the most powerful man never to be king. Much of the fighting actually took place in dense fog.

WARWICK CASTLE

Warwick Castle is one of England's most imposing medieval fortresses. A castle has stood on this sandstone bluff above the River Avon since 1068, but by the 1200s stone walls had replaced the original Norman motte-and-bailey wooden fortress. Later changes included the rebuilt gatehouse, with a barbican in front, and an unfinished tower house, planned in 1478 by Richard of Gloucester to house cannon. Domestic building went on during the reign of Henry VIII, but few changes have been made to the outside of the castle since 1800.

EDWARD V AND RICHARD III: 1483–85

EDWARD V (1483)

EDWARD V, NEVER CROWNED, is remembered as one of the two 'Princes in the Tower'. He was born in 1470, during the Wars of the Roses, when his mother had sought sanctuary in Westminster Abbey and his father Edward IV had fled abroad.

King Edward IV died in April 1483. His brother Richard, Duke of Gloucester, acted swiftly to snatch the young king from his mother's family, the Woodvilles. Young Edward and his brother Richard were lodged in the Tower of London, then a royal residence as well as a prison.

Church, Lords and Commons declared that Edward IV's marriage to Elizabeth Woodville had been illegal – and that his sons were therefore illegitimate. Richard of Gloucester was offered the Crown, and by the autumn the young princes had vanished. Their fate remains a mystery.

RICHARD III (1483–85)

Few kings of England divide opinion more sharply than Richard III. Born at Fotheringhay Castle in 1452, Richard clearly had ability and fought bravely in the Roses wars. He had a dark side – he was probably present at the murder of Henry VI in 1471 – but was also generous and kindly. Marriage to Anne Neville, daughter of the Earl of Warwick, brought Richard land and wealth, especially in northern England where he was a popular and fair governor.

'He came into the world with the feet forward – as men be borne out of it – and (as the fame runs) also not untoothed.'

Sir Thomas More, Tudor historian, on the
'unnatural birth' of Richard III

UNCROWNED KING

Edward V, from a 15th-century painted panel. The crown above (but not on) his head indicates that he was never crowned king.

MURDER MOST ROYAL?

The two princes were seen playing in the Tower garden, and last glimpsed through barred windows. It is probable that the boys were murdered in August 1483. Bones found in 1674 buried in a wooden box (other remains came to light in the 1980s) were buried in Westminster Abbey on the orders of Charles II. The chief suspect (if murder it was) must be Richard III, though some think both Henry Tudor and the Duke of Buckingham also had a motive, with the Crown in their sights.

RICHARD THE KING

This portrait of Richard III by an unknown artist shows no sign of the 'crookback' deformity made much of in later characterizations. Was the artist fearful of showing it or did it not exist?

The Woodvilles feared Richard and he detested them, hence his swift action in April 1483 in removing the fatherless Edward V from the Woodvilles' clutches while the boy travelled under escort from his home in Ludlow to London. Arrests and executions removed Richard's opponents and he was crowned on 6 July.

Rumours that the Princes in the Tower were dead were never scotched, for Richard failed to produce his nephews. He weathered Buckingham's rebellion in 1483, then lost his only son Edward in 1484 and his wife in 1485. Later that year, Henry Tudor, Earl of Richmond, landed in Wales from France to mount his challenge for the throne.

The rivals met at Bosworth Field, where Richard died fighting bravely. The crown he wore so briefly was seized by a new dynasty, the Tudors, and it was their account of 'Richard Crookback' that passed into legend.

THE BATTLE OF BOSWORTH

BY THE SUMMER of 1485 Richard III's mind was troubled and not just by the recent deaths of his son and wife. Gossip was abroad that the king already had his mind set on marrying his niece, Elizabeth of York – to strengthen his grip on the Crown.

But Richard had more than marriage plans to concern him. Across the Channel, Henry Tudor was preparing an invasion. Richard knew of the plans but, since Henry had French backing, could do little to forestall them.

Henry's landing at Milford Haven on 7 August 1485 was greeted enthusiastically by Welsh supporters. Richard was at Nottingham, a good central position from which to confront any invader. As Henry moved eastwards, the king led his forces out to confront him and the two sides met at Sutton Cheney, near Market Bosworth, in Leicestershire.

Although the two armies were fairly evenly matched, on the sidelines waited a third force that was to decide the outcome. These troops from the north were under the command of Lord Stanley and his brother William. Henry tried to win them over, but Richard held Stanley's son hostage and the two brothers had not yet shown their hand. Richard expected the Stanleys to fight for him, but they did not move – until late in the day when their arrival on the flank swung the battle in Henry's favour.

'He came to the field with the crown upon his head that thereby he might either make a beginning or end of his reign.'

Polydore Vergil, Italian historian, writing of Richard III at Bosworth

Betrayed (as he must have seen it) by key allies, Richard fell fighting valiantly, refusing to run when he had the chance. The crown was picked up from a bush, and placed on Henry's head. Richard III's body was stripped and humiliated, the common fate of the loser in medieval war. Trussed on a horse's back, it was carried off for burial in the Church of the Grey Friars, Leicester, with scant respect. Years later, the remains were thrown into the River Soar, though Henry VII ordered an imposing alabaster tomb as a belated monument to the last Yorkist king (a monument that did not survive Henry VIII's dissolution of the monasteries).

Henry VII was now England's king. Richard lay largely unmourned, though York's loyal citizens recorded their grief in the city council minutes: one John Spooner bringing news 'that King Richard late mercifully reigning on us … was piteously slain and murdered to the great heaviness of this city'.

AFTER THE BATTLE

Polydore Vergil described the scene as evening fell on Bosworth Field. **'Henry, after the victory, gave forthwith thanks unto Almighty God …** [and then] commanded his soldiers to cure [care for] the wounded and to bury them that were slain. He gave unto the nobility and gentlemen immortal thanks, promising that he would be mindful of their benefits …'. Henry then packed up his baggage train and made for Leicester, to 'refresh his soldiers from their travails and pains'.

TUDORS

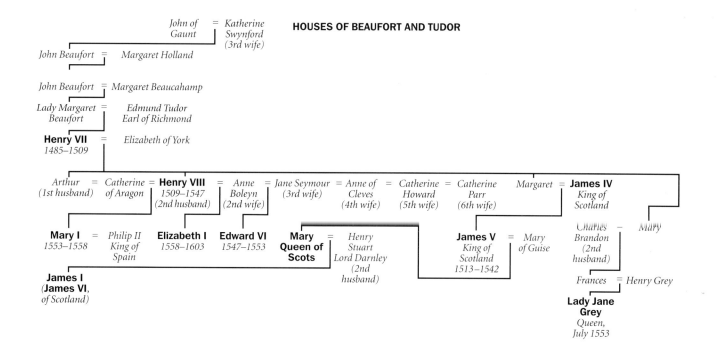

John of Gaunt = Katherine Swynford (3rd wife)

John Beaufort = Margaret Holland

John Beaufort = Margaret Beaucahamp

Lady Margaret Beaufort = Edmund Tudor Earl of Richmond

Henry VII 1485–1509 = Elizabeth of York

Arthur (1st husband) = Catherine of Aragon = **Henry VIII** 1509–1547 (2nd husband) = Anne Boleyn (2nd wife) = Jane Seymour (3rd wife) = Anne of Cleves (4th wife) = Catherine Howard (5th wife) = Catherine Parr (6th wife) ——— Margaret = **James IV** King of Scotland

Mary I 1553–1558 = Philip II King of Spain — **Elizabeth I** 1558–1603 — **Edward VI** 1547–1553 — **Mary Queen of Scots** = Henry Stuart Lord Darnley (2nd husband) — **James V** King of Scotland 1513–1542 = Mary of Guise — Charles Brandon (2nd husband) – Mary

James I (**James VI**, of Scotland)

Frances = Henry Grey

Lady Jane Grey Queen, July 1553

DANGERS AVERTED

A gold medal by Nicholas Hilliard of Queen Elizabeth I, made to celebrate the defeat of the Spanish Armada in 1588.

TWIN BASTIONS AGAINST INVASION

St Mawes Castle in Cornwall was built (1540–43) for King Henry VIII, to protect his realm from French invasion. On the other side of the River Fal is its twin gun-fort, Pendennis Castle.

THE TUDORS REIGNED over England as it transformed from a war-torn medieval kingdom into a dynamic, economically vibrant proto-modern state. For many historians, medieval England ends on Bosworth's battlefield. Henry VII was a 'managerial' monarch; Henry VIII a 'Renaissance man'; Elizabeth I a woman of rare gifts, the inspiration to a nation broadening its horizons through exploration, investigation, innovation and an explosion of artistic talent.

Henry VII, invader turned banker, gave people the peace they needed after decades of civil war. His son Henry VIII dreamed of making England a Continental power and – while he pursued his dynastic ambitions – the English were left to better themselves economically. This was the age of the rising merchant class. Old medieval families found their influence at court challenged by a new breed of counsellors – such as the butcher's son from Ipswich, Thomas Wolsey.

Religion was the new battleground during the upheaval of the Reformation. Quarrels between Protestants and Catholics were mirrored in the conflicting policies of Henry VIII's successors: his three children – Edward VI, Mary I and Elizabeth I. Elizabeth survived plots, perils and attempted overthrow by mighty Spain to reign long and gloriously. Yet there was a final irony. Her father married six times, desperate to secure the Tudor succession, but Elizabeth refused to marry at all. When, old and weary, she died in 1603, next in line for the English throne was the Stuart king of Scotland, James VI. The Tudor dynasty had proved to be a short but spectacular one.

HENRY VII AND HENRY VIII: 1485–1547

HENRY VII (1485–1509)

HENRY TUDOR WAS BORN in 1457. His father Edmund Tudor was already dead and his teenage mother, Margaret Beaufort, soon remarried. Through the Beaufort family line, Henry claimed descent from the Lancastrian 'sire', John of Gaunt.

Flimsy claims to the throne were not unusual during the Wars of the Roses, but needed troops, skill and determination to back them up. Henry led his small force into England in 1485. Victory at Bosworth won him the Crown, and a speedy marriage to Elizabeth of York, daughter of Edward IV, began healing the wounds of a 30-year civil war.

Henry proved prudent, cautious and a financially sound manager. Yorkist upris-ings supported the spurious claims of the harmless Lambert Simnel in 1487, and Perkin Warbeck ten years later. These challenges were ended firmly but without bloodbaths. The king's foreign policy – unadventurous but commercially rewarding – laid the foundations for future Tudor prosperity. For 24 years, Henry VII gave his war-weary land the peace and security it craved.

A WATCHFUL WINNER

Aspects of Henry VII's character emerge sharply in this painting. Calculating and careworn, the man of action who won the throne has become a watchful guardian of it.

HENRY VIII (1509–47)

Henry VIII hijacked English history, yet at his birth in 1491 it seemed unlikely that this second son of Henry VII would ever be king. However, in 1502 his 16-year-old brother Arthur died, leaving Henry to inherit not only Arthur's position as heir to the throne but also his widow Catherine of Aragon as a future wife.

Henry VII died in April 1509. The new king, just 18, was a vigorous contrast to his sober parent. Athletic, intelligent, a scholar,

Henry's campaigns in France achieved frustratingly little, while costing the fortune his father had so carefully amassed. His absence also tempted the Scots to invade – and come to grief at Flodden in 1513. Yet Henry had his successes too. Fascinated by ships and guns, he turned the navy into a powerful fighting force. He won from the Pope the title *Fidei Defensor* (Defender of the Faith) for responding to criticisms of the Church by the Protestant Martin Luther. He picked astute men like Cardinal Wolsey to run his government.

Yet still Henry had no male heir. A daughter, Mary, arrived in 1516, but he needed a legitimate son and Catherine was too old to provide one. Thus began Henry's marriage marathon. His break with Rome paved the way for England to become a Protestant country, although the king continued to think himself a good Catholic. Those who failed to toe Henry's line – including Thomas More, and rebels roused in 1536 by the destruction of the monasteries – were shown no mercy. A bloated, raging tyrant had replaced the much-admired young king.

In 1537 Henry finally had his son, Edward, born to Jane Seymour. The old king died in 1547 having failed to fulfil the golden promise of his youth, yet his legacy was an image of kingship unequalled in English history, and three children – Edward, Mary and Elizabeth – to fulfil the Tudor destiny.

MONARCH OF ALL HE SURVEYS

Henry VIII, the epitome of majestic might in 1537 and rejoicing in the birth of his baby son Edward. The handsome young king was becoming gross with advancing years and declining vigour.

theologian, musician and poet, Henry personified Renaissance Man. Yet he disliked dealing with detail. What Henry saw was the big picture, with himself at the centre.

Henry's two driving ambitions were to rival Europe's foremost leaders – the kings of France and Spain and the Holy Roman Emperor – and to continue the Tudor line by producing an heir. On New Year's Day 1511 he had his heart's desire – a son – but the child was dead within two months. Bitterly disappointed, Henry threw himself into preparing for war, displaying his martial skills at lavish jousting tournaments.

SPORT OF KINGS

Hawking remained a favourite royal pastime in Tudor times, and Henry VIII was often to be found out riding with a hooded hawk on his gloved hand.

CATHERINE OF ARAGON
This stained-glass window shows the queen at prayer. Spanish-born Catherine was intelligent, accomplished and politically astute.

QUEEN'S JEWEL CASE
A 16th-century jewel case, thought to have been Anne Boleyn's. Tall and dark-eyed, Anne played a bold game of coquetry to win her place as Henry's queen.

THE YOUNGEST DAUGHTER of Ferdinand and Isabella of Spain, Catherine of Aragon was well aware that her role as Henry's queen was to bear children. A son arrived in 1511, but sadly lived only a few weeks. Five other pregnancies produced only one surviving child, Mary, in 1516.

Desperate for a son, Henry's affections began to wander and in 1519 his mistress Elizabeth Blount gave birth to a boy, named Henry Fitzroy. Henry possibly had a view to making the boy his heir, since by the 1520s Catherine's hopes of bearing a son were slight. The king became convinced that God was punishing him for marrying his brother Arthur's widow (even though the Pope had given permission) – and he had also fallen in love with Anne Boleyn.

No great beauty, Anne was witty, vivacious and bewitching. She at first resisted Henry's advances but by the end of 1532 was pregnant. Henry demanded a divorce from Catherine, rejecting papal authority and getting Archbishop Cranmer to give him a decree of nullity. His 'great matter' destroyed loyal servants such as Wolsey and Thomas More, while the Act of Supremacy (1534) made him Head of the Church in England.

Henry and Anne married secretly in January 1533 and in September Anne gave birth to a daughter, Elizabeth. Bitterly disappointed, Henry's anguish increased when Anne miscarried twice more, the second time with a son. Anne had failed him. He readily listened to whispers of her adultery with five men (one her brother); Anne was beheaded in May 1536.

Eleven days later, Henry married Jane Seymour, a sweet-natured woman of 27. But the king's joy at their son's birth in October 1537 was short-lived, for his 'entirely beloved' Jane died of childbed fever less than a week later, leaving him grief-stricken.

Henry's fourth marriage, in 1540, was a diplomatic match. He had seen only a portrait of the Protestant princess Anne of Cleves, and was downcast when they met. 'I like her not,' he told Thomas Cromwell. The marriage was not consummated, and a speedy divorce amicably arranged.

Henry's eye next fell on one of Anne's ladies-in-waiting. Catherine Howard, only 19 but already sexually adventurous, was an easy tool of her ambitious family. Nineteen days after his divorce, the ageing king married her. But Catherine's indiscreet amours continued, and when her enemies told the cuckolded Henry, he wept with rage and self-pity. In February 1542, Catherine followed her lovers to the block.

'Divorced, beheaded, died; divorced, beheaded, survived.'

Popular rhyme

GATE OF NO RETURN

In February 1542, Catherine Howard was taken by barge from Hampton Court to the Tower, entering through Traitor's Gate. Her careless flirtations had proved fatal.

'BOUND TO OBEY AND SERVE'

Modest, virtuous Jane Seymour lived up to her family motto. Adept at managing Henry's moods, she gave him the son he had yearned for.

The king married for the last time in July 1543. Catherine Parr was a widow whose motto was: 'To be useful in all I do'. She proved a kind companion-nurse to the ailing monarch, and a caring stepmother to his youngest children, Edward (6) and Elizabeth (10). After Henry's death on 29 January 1547, Catherine married Thomas Seymour, her fourth husband. She bore a daughter but, like Jane Seymour before her, sickened with childbed fever and died shortly afterwards.

GOLDEN DAWN

Henry's reign began in a blaze of glory and flattery – he was 'the handsomest potentate I have ever set eyes on,' according to one ambassador; 'the whole world will talk of him,' cooed another. The first royal wedding was the excuse for a celebration of epic lavish-ness, with magnificent banquets, music, dancing and jousting. **'Our time is spent in continual festival,'** Queen Catherine wrote.

EDWARD VI

The young monarch in this painting has his father's fair hair. Some have seen a likeness to his grandfather, Henry VII.

EDWARD VI (1547–53)

HENRY VIII DIED LEAVING a sickly son, not quite ten, to be tussled over by rival magnates. Edward VI was intelligent and – had he been older and healthier – might have balanced the powerful forces contesting for control of the kingdom. He was entrusted to the care of his uncle, Edward Seymour, who governed England as Protector until 1552 when he was ousted by John Dudley, Earl of Warwick (later Duke of Northumberland).

Both men favoured the religious ideas of the Protestant Reformation, which Henry VIII had kept at bay but which the young king seems to have approved. Cranmer's English Prayer Book of 1549 was a symbol of the new era. Edward died at the age of 16, of consumption, probably made worse by the medical treatments he had been subjected to.

LADY JANE GREY (1553)

Desperate to stop Edward's devoutly Catholic sister Mary from becoming queen, the Duke of Northumberland tried to re-route the Crown to his daughter-in-law Lady Jane Grey, granddaughter of Henry VIII's sister Mary. So anxious had Edward been to preserve the Protestant succession that he had apparently signed a document making cousin Jane his heir. Only 16, Jane was proclaimed queen in London on 9 July 1553, but within days it was clear that the country backed Mary. Although Jane, the nine-days' queen, willingly gave up her unwanted crown, she was tried for treason along with her husband and beheaded in 1554.

CORONATION PROCESSION

Londoners turn out to cheer Edward VI on Coronation Day in 1547. The boy-king had a rather rigorous upbringing (reflected in the number of schools founded in his name), lightened by the good sense and affection of his stepmother Catherine Parr.

'While my father lives I shall be only the Lady Mary, the most unhappy lady in Christendom.'

Mary I, lamenting being unmarried at 28 years old

MARY I (1553–58)

Edward's enthusiastic Protestant beliefs were not shared by his older sister Mary. Declared a bastard when Henry VIII put aside her mother, Catherine of Aragon, Mary believed her task was to restore England to Catholicism – 'the true faith'.

Having managed to evade marriage with Thomas Seymour, England's Lord Admiral, Mary chose as husband in 1554 the most severe Catholic ruler in Europe, Philip of Spain. Her action outraged some Protestants who, led by Sir Thomas Wyatt, staged a short-lived, futile rebellion. The Duke of Suffolk – Lady Jane Grey's father – joined the rebellion and so sealed poor Jane's fate.

Mary longed for a child but, like her father, endured disappointment. Soon wearying of her, and of the English, Philip went home to Spain while the queen vented her resentment on 'heretics': the Protestant bishops Ridley and Latimer, who were burned at the stake in 1555, and Archbishop Cranmer in 1556. These, and some 300 other victims, caused people to call the queen 'Bloody Mary', and the loss in 1558 of Calais, England's last possession in France, was viewed as a national disgrace.

Loveless, stubborn Mary presents a sad figure. Only in her final months, wracked by illness, was she reconciled with her sister Elizabeth (17 years her junior), whom she had accused of plotting against her. When Mary died on 17 November 1558, Elizabeth heard the news at Hatfield. 'This is the Lord's doing; it is marvellous in our eyes,' she said, quoting the Psalms.

MARY I

A precocious child, Mary was adored by her father Henry VIII – but rejected when he divorced her mother. Her religious intolerance led to persecution of Protestants.

ELIZABETH I (1558–1603)

ELIZABETH, DAUGHTER OF HENRY VIII and Anne Boleyn, was born at Greenwich on 7 September 1533. When her mother was executed three years later, the little princess was banished from court as an unwanted bastard, but restored to the family by Henry's sixth wife, Catherine Parr.

QUEEN ENTHRONED

Elizabeth in her coronation robes, with orb and sceptre. Her accession was greeted with joy by court and common people alike.

Elizabeth survived a perilous childhood and adolescence, seen for a time by her sister Queen Mary as a potential threat. But, shrewd and tenacious, she proved a long-time survivor, gaining the throne at 24 and reigning until her 70th year through times both troubled and triumphant.

Henry's daughter had a first-class mind, sharpened by an excellent education. Musical, well-read and athletic, she gloried in dancing and hunting. Her father's pride and energy – as well as his fiery hair and temper – combined with her mother's coquettishness and magnetism. Yet early in life she learned to be cautious, avoiding confrontation whenever possible. Although the resulting ambiguity often exasperated her courtiers, on major issues she was usually crystal clear. She faltered only once, over the fate of her potential rival, Mary Queen of Scots – executed in 1587.

BY ROYAL COMMAND

The queen enjoyed the theatre. In 1575 she had visited Kenilworth Castle for three weeks of pageantry, a spectacle that the young William Shakespeare (then 11) may have been brought to see. By 1592, Shakespeare was in London, and his plays were performed before the queen, as well as in the splendid new Globe Theatre, London's finest, opened in 1599. Elizabeth is said to have enjoyed the character of Falstaff (in *Henry IV Parts 1 and 2*) so much that the playwright wrote the 'Fat Knight' into a new comedy – *The Merry Wives of Windsor*.

'The Queen would
like everyone to be
in love with her…'

Comment by a foreign
ambassador in London

CARRIED BY HER KNIGHTS

*The queen carried in procession
to Blackfriars by six Knights of
the Garter; a painting attributed
to Robert Peake the Elder,
c. 1600. Elizabeth's summer
'progresses' around the kingdom
were even grander, incurring
colossal entertainment expenses.*

A MERRY DANCE

*Elizabeth was never without
favourites; Robert Dudley (seen
here dancing with the queen)
she loved the best, but
Christopher Hatton, Walter
Raleigh and Robert Devereux,
Earl of Essex, also danced to her
tunes, though none ruled her.*

Elizabeth's court was seldom dull: 'When she smiled it was pure sunshine … but anon came a storm and thunder fell in a wondrous manner on all alike.' She put her trust in wisely-chosen chief ministers who served her well: the lawyer William Cecil (Lord Burghley) and his son Robert, aided by Sir Francis Walsingham, spy-master and intelligence chief.

For years, the queen's choice of husband was a hot topic throughout Europe, but the only man she came near to accepting was her 'Little Frog', the clever and amusing Duke of Alençon. Marriage held too many pitfalls – and loss of independence. In the end prudence or fear held her back. She remained 'the Virgin Queen', taking pride in the deeds of Francis Drake and his fellow sea dogs, and delighting in the flattery of her illustrious playwrights and poets. The defeat of Spain's Armada in 1588 was the high point of her reign, occasioning an ecstasy of patriotic fervour with a semi-divine queen, 'Gloriana', at its centre.

In the spring of 1603, she caught a chill. 'To content the people, you must go to bed,' urged Robert Cecil. 'Little man, is "must" a word to be addressed to princes?' was her acidly genial response. She died at Richmond on 24 March 1603, and with her ended not just the Tudor dynasty, but the richly patterned 'golden age' of English history that carries Elizabeth's name.

59

THE ARMADA

'I know I have the body of a weak and feeble woman, but I have the heart and stomach of a king …'

Elizabeth I speaking to her army at Tilbury before the Armada's approach

ENGLAND HAD BEEN SLOW to join Europe's maritime adventure, begun in the 1400s by Portuguese and Spanish ships sailing to America and around Africa to India and China. Henry VII had sponsored the Cabots' voyages of exploration, and Henry VIII had delighted in bigger and better warships, like the *Mary Rose*. But it was Elizabeth's sea captains who from the 1560s poured riches into the royal coffers by a combination of trade and piracy. Many of the adventurers – among them

Walter Raleigh, John Hawkins, Martin Frobisher and Francis Drake – were also those called to defend England against the Armada from Spain in 1588.

Philip of Spain, obsessed with a mission to restore England to the true Catholic faith, ordered the largest invasion fleet ever seen. He had hopes of a pro-Catholic uprising to welcome his ships, laden with battle-hardened troops ready to drive Elizabeth from her throne. Along the

FINISH THE GAME

Drake plays bowls on Plymouth Hoe while the English fleet awaits the signal that the Armada is in sight.

THE ARMADA PORTRAIT

A painting of Queen Elizabeth, now at Woburn Abbey, known as the 'Armada' portrait. Through one window the Armada can be seen; through the other, the storm that scattered England's foes.

south coast of England, beacons were built to flame into life when lookouts signalled the first sail of the Spanish fleet.

Spain's captains were tough and experienced, but their huge galleons were slow and lumbering, unsuited to the Channel's tricky tides and currents. Smaller and faster, the English ships had much better gunnery; above all, English sailors knew their own winds, tides and shallows.

Commanding the English fleet was Lord Howard of Effingham, whose job was to control and coordinate the swashbuckling captains of his fighting ships. English vessels harried the Armada, sailing majestically up the Channel towards a rendezvous with the Duke of Parma's invasion army at Calais. The Spanish pushed on doggedly, desperate to tackle the English at close quarters but – anchored off the coast of France – were surprised by English fireships and almost driven on shore during a hectic skirmish off Gravelines. The Channel weather then took a hand as winds blew the Spanish ships back out to sea, but northwards. The tattered fleet made for home via Scotland and Ireland – suffering terrible losses from savage storms. Of 130 ships that left Spain, fewer than half returned; more than 10,000 Spanish perished. The English lost not a single ship.

THE SPANISH ARMADA
AT GRAVELINES

This painting in the National Maritime Museum at Greenwich is thought to be a contemporary record. The Armada galleons are being attacked by smaller English ships, and one (top left), is sinking.

61

KINGS AND QUEENS
OF SCOTLAND

OVERLOOKING AULD REEKIE

The castle, Edinburgh's most striking landmark, stands on a basalt rock above the city. The oldest part of the castle is St Margaret's Chapel, built for the wife of Malcolm III in the 11th century.

SCOTTISH AND ENGLISH MONARCHS had been linked by many centuries of war, inter-marriage and diplomacy. Pre-medieval Scotland was a mix of peoples. North of the Forth were the Picts, or 'painted people', who fought the Romans in the 1st century AD. Later, people from Dalriada (Antrim) in Ireland settled in Argyll. These were the Scots, whose language developed into Gaelic. Other peoples included Angles in Lothian and Britons in Strathclyde. The uneasy balance between Picts, Britons, Scots and English was threatened in the 800s by invasions of Vikings from Scandinavia, and though in 843 Kenneth MacAlpin became ruler of both Picts and Scots in a kingdom known as Scotia, Viking attacks continued. Gradually, all peoples in Scotland came under the rule of the King of Scots.

KING OF SCOTS

Alexander III crowned at Scone, in a 15th-century manuscript. The ceremony, in the presence of seven lords and seven bishops, ended with the king being hailed in Gaelic.

After 1066 the Normans forced weaker Scottish kings to become their vassals and introduced Anglo-Norman feudal ways as well as their language. While some Scottish rulers were under the thumb of more power-ful English kings, others were their rivals in prestige and majesty. Wars of resistance in the late 1200s and early 1300s, inspired by William Wallace and Robert the Bruce, threw off the English yoke laid on the Scots by Edward I and Edward III. Scotland emerged as a proudly independent kingdom under the Stuart (originally Stewart) kings. Relations with England, as with France, remained close through diplomatic marriages, and so it was that in 1603 James VI of Scotland found himself travelling south, much pleased, to become James I of England.

THE LION KING

Robert the Bruce as a lion, surrounded by shields of his main supporters. From a decorated communal drinking cup called the Bute Mazer.

STONE OF SCONE

The Stone of Destiny, seen here with the Honours of Scotland, is said to have arrived in Scotland around the year 500 with Fergus Mor mac Erc. It was moved to Scone by Kenneth MacAlpin in 843 for his coronation and successive kings of Scotland were crowned upon it.

HOUSES OF ALPIN AND DUNKELD: 843-1058

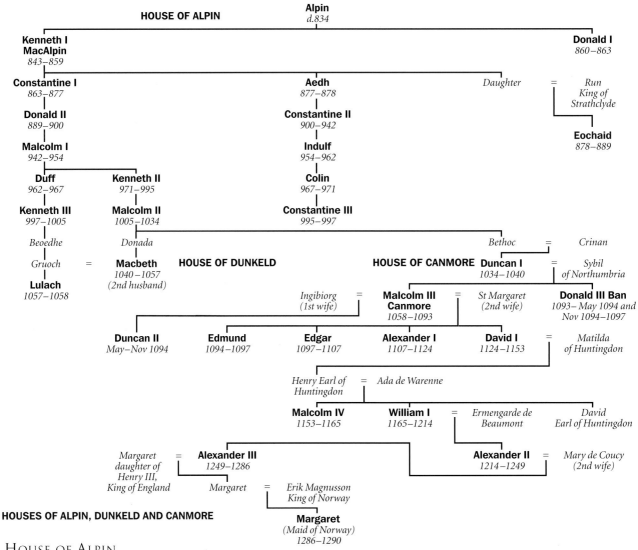

HOUSE OF ALPIN

Alpin
d.834

Kenneth I MacAlpin
843–859

Donald I
860–863

Constantine I
863–877

Aedh
877–878

Daughter = *Run King of Strathclyde*

Donald II
889–900

Constantine II
900–942

Eochaid
878–889

Malcolm I
942–954

Indulf
954–962

Duff
962–967

Kenneth II
971–995

Colin
967–971

Kenneth III
997–1005

Malcolm II
1005–1034

Constantine III
995–997

Bethoc = *Crinan*

Beoedhe

Donada

HOUSE OF DUNKELD

HOUSE OF CANMORE

Duncan I
1034–1040
= *Sybil of Northumbria*

Gruoch = **Macbeth**
1040–1057
(2nd husband)

Ingibiorg (1st wife) = **Malcolm III Canmore**
1058–1093
= *St Margaret (2nd wife)*

Donald III Ban
1093– May 1094 and Nov 1094–1097

Lulach
1057–1058

Duncan II
May–Nov 1094

Edmund
1094–1097

Edgar
1097–1107

Alexander I
1107–1124

David I
1124–1153
= *Matilda of Huntingdon*

Henry Earl of Huntingdon = *Ada de Warenne*

Malcolm IV
1153–1165

William I
1165–1214
= *Ermengarde de Beaumont*

David Earl of Huntingdon

Margaret daughter of Henry III, King of England = **Alexander III**
1249–1286

Alexander II
1214–1249
= *Mary de Coucy (2nd wife)*

Margaret = *Erik Magnusson King of Norway*

HOUSES OF ALPIN, DUNKELD AND CANMORE

Margaret
(Maid of Norway)
1286–1290

HOUSE OF ALPIN
KENNETH MACALPIN (843–59)

IN 834, A BATTLE involving Alpin, King of the Dalriada Scots, and Eoghann, King of the Picts, left both leaders dead. The man who proved strong enough to enforce a claim to both kingdoms was Kenneth MacAlpin, son of the Scots king and descended through his mother from the Pictish royal house. In 843 he became ruler of the Picts and Scots in a Celtic kingdom known as Scotia.

MacAlpin moved the centre of his kingdom to Pictland, setting the ancient Stone of Destiny in Scone, where he was crowned. Gaelic speech spread north of the Forth and Pictish (like Celtic but with traces of an ancient language unrelated to others in Europe) disappeared.

Royal succession among the Picts was matrilineal (through the mother). Kenneth MacAlpin chose the Scottish system of succession – tanistry – by which an heir was selected during the old king's lifetime. This system lasted until Malcolm II, final king of the House of Alpin, replaced it with the principle of direct descent.

MALCOLM II (1005–34)

In the late 800s and 900s, Vikings overran Northumbria, leaving its northern province of Lothian easy prey for the Scots. The shrewd, ruthless Malcolm II brought Lothian into Scotia with his victory over the Northumbrians at Carham in 1018. Around the same time he put his grandson Duncan on the throne of the British kingdom of Strathclyde. The union of all Scotland was prepared and, having no son, Malcolm cleared the way for Duncan to succeed him by murdering the grandson of Kenneth III.

HOUSE OF DUNKELD
DUNCAN I (1034–40)

Malcolm's grandson Duncan, born around 1001, was the first monarch of a united Scotland. His two sons – Malcolm Canmore and Donald Ban – had their hereditary right to the throne threatened when Duncan's cousin Macbeth claimed the kingdom on grounds of tanistry. This dynastic wrangling was settled when Macbeth killed Duncan in battle near Elgin in 1040.

MACBETH (1040–57)

Born around 1005, Macbeth – another grandson of Malcolm II – seems to have reigned successfully for 17 years. His wife Gruoch, granddaughter of Kenneth III, had a son called Lulach by a previous marriage. Defeated by Malcolm Canmore at Scone in 1054, Macbeth was then killed by him at Lumphanan in 1057 and was succeeded by his stepson Lulach. Shakespeare adapted the facts freely for his play about the Scottish king.

LULACH (THE FOOL) (1057–58)

Macbeth's stepson ruled for just a few months before being killed at Strathbogie by Malcolm Canmore.

GLAMIS CASTLE

In Shakespeare's 'Scottish play', the first witch hails Macbeth as 'thane of Glamis'; the castle dates from the 15th century, and was subsequently much altered in the French style.

MELROSE ABBEY

Founded by Cistercian monks beside the Tweed in 1136, with the support of King David I, Melrose became one of the richest abbeys in Scotland. Sheep farming provided much of its income.

MALCOLM III (CANMORE) (1058–93)

HIS RIVALS DISPOSED OF, Malcolm (born around 1031) gained the throne. Canmore (Gaelic *ceann Mor*) means 'big head' or 'great chief'. After the defeat of his father, Duncan, Malcolm had fled to Anglo-Saxon Northumbria. In England he may have met Margaret, sister of the ousted English heir Edgar Atheling, for in 1069 he married her as his second wife. With her came English fashions and customs. Saxon supplanted Gaelic at the Scots court and a kind of feudalism replaced the clan system. Malcolm invaded England several times but in 1072 was forced to submit to William the Conqueror who had marched into Scotland. In 1093, on his fifth raid into England, Malcolm was killed at Alnwick.

DONALD III BAN (1093–94)

Malcolm's brother Donald Ban, born around 1033, led the resistance to 'southern' influence, and claimed the throne on grounds of tanistry. He was ousted a year later by Duncan, Malcolm's son by his first wife.

DUNCAN II (MAY–NOVEMBER 1094)

Duncan's backer was William Rufus, Norman king of England, who became a close friend when the Scot was held hostage at the English court. Seen as an English vassal, Duncan was unpopular. His stepbrother Edmund and Donald Ban defeated and killed him at Mondynes.

DONALD BAN AND EDMUND (1094–97)

Edmund – one of Malcolm Canmore's six sons by Margaret – ruled in Lothian and Strathclyde while Donald Ban reigned in Scotia. But Edmund's brother Edgar enlisted an English army to overthrow the twin kings. Edmund, pardoned, became a monk. Donald Ban was blinded and imprisoned for life.

EDGAR (THE PEACEABLE) (1097–1107)

Born about 1074, Malcolm and Margaret's fourth son gained his derisory nickname from his submissive attitude to England, grant of the Western Isles to Norway and encouragement of Anglo-Normans into Scotland. Having moved the royal residence from Dunfermline to

Edinburgh, this unmarried monarch left the kingdom to his brothers Alexander and David.

ALEXANDER I (THE FIERCE) (1107–24)

Born around 1077, Alexander married an illegitimate daughter of England's Henry I and gained his nickname from ferociously subduing an uprising in Moray. Technically an English vassal, he championed Scottish identity, especially in Church matters.

DAVID I (1124–53)

Sixth (and last) of Malcolm and Margaret's sons, born around 1080, David I was one of the greatest Scottish kings. Marrying a granddaughter of Northumbria's Earl Siward gave him claim to a large part of northern England. Raised in England at Henry I's court, he took full advantage of the struggle between the king's daughter Matilda and her cousin Stephen. On Henry's death he marched into England, taking Carlisle and Newcastle before his defeat at the Battle of the Standard, near Northallerton, in 1138. Stephen yielded him control of Northumbria.

David transformed Scotland into a feudal society, with Anglo-Norman tenants; new royal burghs; the first Scottish coinage; and monastic centres (including Melrose and Holyrood). He imposed Norman law, established a feudal court and the office of Chancellor. With the death of his only son in 1152, David appointed his 11-year-old grandson Malcolm to succeed him.

HOLYROOD ABBEY
The abbey was founded in 1128 by David I, who (the story goes) escaped from a maddened stag when a cross miraculously materialized between the king and the animal. Very little survives of the original building.

ST MARGARET'S CHAPEL
Edinburgh's oldest surviving building, dedicated to the memory of Queen Margaret, wife of Malcolm Canmore, by her son David I. The queen died here, on the rock of Edinburgh Castle, in 1093.

THE PEARL OF SCOTLAND

Queen Margaret, mother of David I, bore six sons – three of whom became kings of Scotland. She spent long hours in prayer in the chapel (now known as St Margaret's Chapel) in the highest part of Edinburgh Castle. Margaret was made a saint in 1251.

LATER HOUSE OF CANMORE: 1153–1290

DOUBLE CROWN

David I and his grandson Malcolm IV, from an illuminated initial letter on Kelso Abbey's charter (granted in 1159). David made monastic reforms and founded new church sees. His grandson inherited the Crown at the age of 11.

MALCOLM IV (THE MAIDEN) (1153–65)

BORN IN 1142, a year before Henry II became King of England, Malcolm was forced in 1157 to renounce his rights to Northumbria. His nickname refers to his vow of chastity.

WILLIAM (THE LION) (1165–1214)

Born in 1143, he succeeded his brother, invaded England in 1174, and was defeated and captured at Alnwick. Imprisoned in Normandy, William was freed in return for accepting Henry II as Scotland's overlord. Ten thousand merks for Richard I's Third Crusade bought back Scotland's sovereignty in 1189. A further 15,000 merks was supposed to secure King John's sons as husbands for William's two daughters. A bad bargain, it was broken by the English king.

'Oure gold was changed into lede.'

Part of a Scots lament on the death of Alexander III

FAIR AND FOUL

The lowland districts were esteemed for their **'green meadows'**, good for farming, but according to the 14th-century chronicler John Fordun, the highlands produced only oats and barley, and were **'very hideous, interspersed with moors and marshy fields, muddy and dirty ... '**. Nevertheless, Scotland abounded in sheep and horses and was **'manifold in its wealth of fish, in sea, river and lake'**.

ALEXANDER II (1214–49)

Son of William the Lion, Alexander was born in 1198. On his accession, King John declared he would 'hunt the red fox cub from his den'. Instead, Alexander backed the barons who forced John to sign Magna Carta in 1215. On marrying Joan, John's daughter, he demanded repayment of William the Lion's dowry and Scottish rights to Northumbria. Diplomacy fixed the border with England at the Tweed-Solway line.

ALEXANDER III (1249–86)

Aged eight on inheriting the throne, Alexander was ten when he married Henry III's 11-year-old daughter Margaret in 1251. Cleverly avoiding the issue of English feudal superiority, he established good relations with King Edward I.

In a golden age of prosperity, towns like Berwick grew rich on foreign trade. Wool, fur and fish were exported. Churches and castles were built. The Western Isles were won back from Norway at the Battle of Largs in 1263. Then in 1275 tragedy struck as the king lost first his wife and soon afterwards their three children. He married again in 1285 but the following year on a stormy night his horse stumbled, tossing him over a cliff to his death. Heir to the Scottish throne was Alexander's three-year-old granddaughter, Margaret, 'Maid of Norway'.

GOLDEN KING

Alexander III's reign was seen by later Scots as a golden age. In 1278 he visited Edward I's court, but did homage only for his lands in England.

DRYBURGH ABBEY

Founded in 1150 by the saintly King David I, this abbey, like others, fell victim to Scotland's border wars with England.

MARGARET, MAID OF NORWAY

This portrait by William Hole, painted about 1900, shows a romanticized version of Margaret, who was just six years old when she died. The portrait is part of a mural in the Scottish National Portrait Gallery.

MARGARET (MAID OF NORWAY) (1286–90)

Margaret's father was Erik II of Norway. Her mother, Alexander III's daughter Margaret, had died giving birth. When the child became Queen of Scotland in 1286, England's Edward I was quick to arrange a marriage between her and his son. But Margaret died – from seasickness, in Orkney – on the journey from Norway and with 'the Maid' died the House of Canmore.

WARS OF INDEPENDENCE

KNEELING TO THE ENEMY

John Balliol pays homage to Edward I of England on 26 December 1292. Edward claimed overlordship of Scotland.

'For it is not glory, it is not riches, neither is it honours but it is freedom alone that we fight and contend for ... '

Declaration of Arbroath

VICTORY AT STIRLING BRIDGE, 1297

Wallace used skilful tactics to defeat the superior English forces, cutting off the cavalry from the main army as they crossed the narrow bridge. Many knights were trapped between the river and Scottish spears.

AFTER ALEXANDER III'S DEATH in 1286, Scotland was plunged into dynastic strife with 13 claimants to the throne. England's powerful Edward I tried to take advantage of Scottish turmoil. Asked to pick a king, he chose John Balliol, great-grandson of David I.

JOHN BALLIOL (1292–96)

In 1292 a Scots king sat on the Stone of Destiny for the last time. John Balliol (born *c.*1250) had affirmed Edward I as his overlord, but after three years he rebelled, only to be crushed by an invading English army at Dunbar, where 10,000 Scots perished. Edward removed the Stone of Destiny and Balliol had the royal arms stripped from his tunic, earning him the mocking title of 'Toom Tabard' ('empty coat'). Freed from a spell in the Tower in 1299, Balliol died in Normandy in 1315.

William Wallace

John de Warenne, Earl of Surrey, was appointed Guardian of Scotland, but the Scots chafed against English rule. Enter the landless second son of an obscure Scottish knight, William Wallace.

Thousands flocked to join Wallace, outlawed for murder. He defeated the English at the Battle of Stirling Bridge, and then led a pillaging expedition into England. In 1298 he was appointed Guardian of Scotland.

Wallace refused the Crown, while reorganizing his army to meet the expected onslaught from Edward I. The crucial battle was at Falkirk, where Wallace's infantry was battered to defeat by English cavalry. Two bitter rivals – Robert Bruce, 2nd Earl of Carrick, and John Comyn (the Red), nephew of Balliol – succeeded Wallace as joint Guardians. Neither had any liking for Wallace, who vanished from the scene until 1305, when he was betrayed and taken prisoner near Glasgow. He was put to death in London, but the war was not yet over.

Robert the Bruce

Born in 1274, Bruce was the great-great-grandson of David I. In 1306, he tried to heal his breach with Comyn, but Comyn told Edward of their agreement, and Bruce narrowly escaped capture by the English. Bruce met Comyn in Greyfriars Church, Dumfries, where he stabbed his rival to death. Declaring himself King of Scotland and its 500,000 or so inhabitants, he was crowned at Scone in 1306.

As Edward I advanced against the Scots, Bruce took to the hills and islands (the legend of the king and the spider dates from this time). Waging a guerrilla war, he defeated the English troops at Glen Trool and Louden Hill. Then in July 1307, Edward died and the English troops were withdrawn, leaving only the garrisoned castles. The Scots retook these one by one, until by 1314 Stirling was the only Scottish castle in English hands. Victory at Bannockburn in 1314 over Edward II's much larger army confirmed Bruce's triumph.

Bruce the Fugitive

In the winter of 1306/7 Bruce and his men lived as outlaws, often hiding in caves, and it is in such a cave that the legend of the king and the spider is set. Bruce, on the point of despair, is said to have watched a spider trying to spin a web. Six times it failed before it succeeded. Bruce was inspired to carry on his campaign against the English.

Scotland's guardian
Wallace stands at Bemersyde, east of Melrose.

Scottish foot soldiers in battle
This 19th-century mural of Bannockburn, by William Hole, shows Scottish infantry with their long spears at close quarters with the English cavalry.

HOUSE OF BRUCE
ROBERT I (THE BRUCE) (1306–29)

IN 1312, THE DECLARATION OF ARBROATH affirmed
Scottish independence and after Edward III came to
the English throne in 1327, Bruce's army harassed the
English until Edward also acknowledged Scottish
sovereignty. A dying man by 1328, Bruce asked
Sir James Douglas to take his heart to the Holy Land
when his body was buried in Dunfermline Abbey. But
Douglas was killed in Spain, and the heart was brought
back for burial in Melrose Abbey.

DAVID II (1329–71)

Married at four years old to Edward II's daughter Joan,
Bruce's son David became King of Scotland a year later.
When he was defeated near Perth in 1332 by Edward
Balliol (son of 'Toom Tabard' and vassal of Edward III of
England) the English king was delighted. Crowned king,
Balliol was promptly thrown out by nobles loyal to David
but a year later he was back and David fled to France.
The Scots rallied under Robert Stewart, Bruce's grand-
son. David returned to Scotland in 1339, and in 1346
invaded England, where he was held prisoner until
1357, becoming friendly with Edward III. As David left
no heir, the Crown passed on his death to the Stewarts,
who took their name from the hereditary title of
Walter, High Steward of Scotland under David I.
Robert Stewart became king at the age of 54.

HOUSE OF STEWART
ROBERT II (THE STEWARD) (1371–90)

Robert ruled as Guardian of Scotland during the absence
of David II but – unlike David – he produced a large
family of 21 children (13 legitimate). In 1384 he wearily
decreed that his eldest son should take over and rule on
his behalf.

ROBERT THE BRUCE AT BANNOCKBURN
*The Scottish hero's statue at the battlefield where he defeated
Edward II's army in 1307.*

ROBERT III (1390–1406)

Robert III was born in 1327 (his real name was John, but he thought Robert sounded more martial). Disabled by a kick from his horse, he was overshadowed by his forceful brother, Robert, Duke of Albany (who may have been behind the death of the king's son David). To protect his second son James, Robert prudently sent the 11-year-old boy to France in 1405 but English pirates kidnapped him. After Robert died in 1406, Albany became Governor until 1420, when his incompetent son Murdoch succeeded him.

JAMES I (1406–37)

James was kept prisoner in England for 18 years, though recognized as king by the Scottish Parliament in 1406. Ransomed in 1424, he returned to Scotland, where he restored order and respect for the monarchy. Conspirators acting for Walter, son of Robert II's second marriage, murdered James I at Perth in 1437.

JAMES II (1437–60)

Six-year-old James II was crowned at Holyrood Abbey – ending the Scone tradition begun by Kenneth MacAlpin. During the childhood of 'James of the Fiery Face' (he had a birthmark), Scotland was ruled by Chancellor Sir William Crichton and Governor Sir Alexander Livingstone. Fear of a Douglas coup was removed at the infamous Black Dinner of 1440 when William, 6th Earl of Douglas (great-grandson of Robert III), was murdered in front of James. Twelve years later the king himself stabbed William, 8th Earl of Douglas, and later defeated the Douglases at Arkholm. While supporting Henry VI in England's Wars of the Roses, James was killed by an exploding cannon at the siege of Roxburgh Castle.

IACOBVS · I · D · GRAT REX · SCOTORVM

IACOBVS 2 D·GRATIA REX · SCOTORVM

JAMES 'THE LAWGIVER'

James I spent 18 years as a prisoner of the English. A great benefactor of St Andrew's University, his crackdown on rebel nobles and reforms made him many enemies.

JAMES 'THE FIERY'

Having removed the Douglases by murder, James II proceeded to improve government and justice in Scotland. No birthmark appears on James' face, perhaps at the artist's discretion.

' *… the worst of kings and the most miserable of men.*'

Robert III's view of himself, expressed to his wife

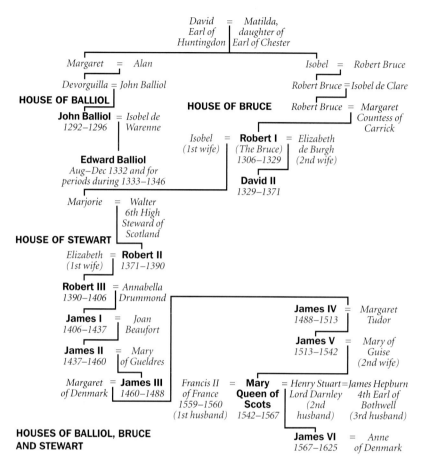

David = Matilda,
Earl of | daughter of
Huntingdon | Earl of Chester

Margaret = Alan .... Isobel = Robert Bruce

Devorguilla = John Balliol .... Robert Bruce = Isobel de Clare

HOUSE OF BALLIOL .... **HOUSE OF BRUCE** .... Robert Bruce = Margaret
Countess of
Carrick

John Balliol = Isobel de .... Isobel = **Robert I** = Elizabeth
1292–1296 | *Warenne* .... (1st wife) | (The Bruce) | de Burgh
.... *1306–1329* | (2nd wife)

Edward Balliol
Aug–Dec 1332 and for
periods during 1333–1346 .... **David II**
1329–1371

Marjorie = Walter
6th High
Steward of
Scotland

HOUSE OF STEWART

Elizabeth = **Robert II**
(1st wife) | *1371–1390*

Robert III = Annabella
1390–1406 | Drummond

James I = Joan .... **James IV** = Margaret
1406–1437 | Beaufort .... *1488–1513* | Tudor

James II = Mary .... **James V** = Mary of
1437–1460 | of Gueldres .... *1513–1542* | Guise
.... (2nd wife)

Margaret = **James III** .... Francis II = **Mary** = Henry Stuart = James Hepburn
of Denmark | *1460–1488* .... of France | **Queen of** | Lord Darnley | 4th Earl of
.... *1559–1560* | **Scots** | (2nd | Bothwell
.... (1st husband) | *1542–1567* | husband) | (3rd husband)

HOUSES OF BALLIOL, BRUCE
AND STEWART .... **James VI** = Anne
.... *1567–1625* | of Denmark

SAINTLY COMPANY

*James III with St Andrew in Hugo van der
Goes' Trinity College altarpiece of 1476.*

JAMES III (1460–88)

BORN IN 1451, JAMES III was still a child when crowned in
Kelso Abbey. His mother Marie of Gueldres ruled as
regent until her death in 1463, after which her son fell
under the influence of the Boyd family until his marriage
in 1469 to Margaret of Denmark. The king's brothers –
Alexander, Duke of Albany and John, Earl of Mar – were
arrested in 1479, suspected of plotting against him. Mar
died suspiciously. Albany escaped to England, where
Edward IV recognized him as King Alexander IV in 1482.
James's bisexuality outraged the Scottish lords; they
hanged one royal boyfriend and when James tried to give
another an earldom, they rallied behind the king's reluctant 15-year-old son James. Father and son met at the
Battle of Sauchieburn near Stirling, where James III lost
the Crown and his life.

JAMES IV (1488–1513)

James IV wore an iron waist chain as penance for the
death of his father. In his reign – marked by a glittering
court – university education flourished, printing was
introduced and a navy established. Though the king
supported the Yorkist pretender Perkin Warbeck against
Henry VII of England, in 1503 he married Henry's
daughter Margaret Tudor. Bound by the 'auld alliance'
to France, James faced a dilemma when Henry VIII
invaded France. The Scottish king led his army across
the border, where he and it were crushed at Flodden,
on 9 September 1513.

THE KING WHO DIED
OF GRIEF

James V – who died after learning of the Scots' defeat at Solway Moss – pictured with his second wife Mary of Guise, mother of Mary Queen of Scots.

'The Flowers of the Forest that fought aye the foremost,
The prime of our land lie cauld in the clay.'

'The Flowers of the Forest' (on the Scots' defeat at Flodden), Jean Elliott

JAMES V (1513–42)

James V was still a baby when crowned at Stirling and this inevitably meant a struggle between his mother Margaret (and her second husband Archibald Douglas, 6th Earl of Angus) on the one hand and John Stuart, Duke of Albany (the nobles' choice as Governor), on the other. Albany left Scotland in 1524, and James fell into the hands of the Douglases until he escaped in 1528 and drove his step-father out of Scotland. James liked to travel incognito among his poorer subjects, but was suspicious of the nobility, whose power he tried to curb. He generously supported the Catholic Church at a time when the Protestant Reformation was gathering momentum.

James sided with France against Henry VIII's England. In 1542 Henry sent an army to Scotland, whereupon the Scots nobles revenged themselves on James by deserting him when the armies clashed at Solway Moss. News of his army's defeat devastated the Scottish king, who died in despair a week after the birth of his daughter Mary (later Queen of Scots). Mary was nine months old when crowned at Stirling Castle in 1543. Her French mother Mary of Guise became regent in 1554, but was defeated by Protestant forces and died in Edinburgh Castle.

FALKLAND PALACE

Built in French Renaissance style between 1501 and 1541 for James IV and James V, Falkland was a favourite residence of the kings while hunting in the forests of Fife.

MARY QUEEN OF SCOTS AND JAMES VI: 1542–1603

'You will do me great good in withdrawing me from this world out of which I am very glad to go.'

Mary Queen of Scots, when told
of her execution date in 1587

DARNLEY'S MURDER SCENE

This contemporary sketch shows Darnley's house at Kirk o' Field after the gunpowder explosion intended to kill him. The bodies of the strangled earl and his servant were in a nearby field.

MARY, BORN IN 1542, was the daughter of Mary of Guise and King James V of Scotland. Her father remarked gloomily at her birth, 'Adieu, farewell, it came with a lass, it will pass with a lass,' – a reference to his family's royal origins in the marriage of Marjory Bruce to Walter Stewart in the early 1300s. James was to die six days later.

In 1548 Mary was sent to France, her mother's homeland, where as a Catholic princess she married the Dauphin Francis in 1558 and the following year became Queen of France. But Francis died in 1560 and Mary returned to Scotland, where she was harangued by the anti-Catholic cleric John Knox. Five years later she married Henry Stuart, Lord Darnley. Though handsome, Darnley was weak and jealous, and

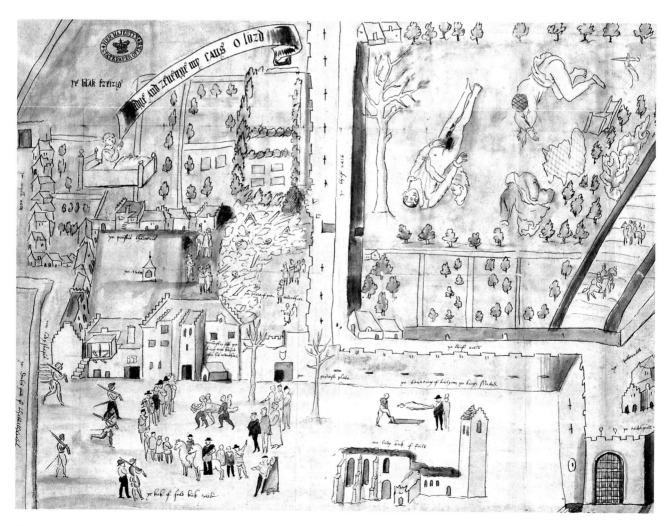

in 1566 he organized the murder of Mary's Italian secretary, David Rizzio.

In February 1567, Darnley himself was murdered. Suspicion fell on the Earl of Bothwell, who made off with Mary (reportedly 'ravishing' her). Three months later they were married. Such a murky business stained Mary's reputation and, confronted by enraged Scottish nobles, she was forced to give up the throne. On 25 July her young son by Darnley was crowned James VI at Stirling, with the Earl of Moray acting as regent. Bothwell fled to Denmark, dying insane in 1578; Mary escaped from Lochleven Castle to seek safety in England.

What was England's Queen Elizabeth to do with her unwanted guest? For 18 years she held on to Mary, who – knowingly or not – became the focus for any plot against her English cousin. Incriminating letters linked her in 1586 with the Babington Plot to murder the English queen, and her fate was sealed. Found guilty of treason, she was beheaded on 6 February 1587. In 1612 her son James had her remains moved from Peterborough Cathedral for reburial in Westminster Abbey.

James's Protestant tutor, George Buchanan, had done his best to portray Mary as evil incarnate, though James rejected this caricature. At 16 he took up the reins of power in Scotland, making friendly overtures to Elizabeth I but doing nothing beyond the diplomatically formal to save his mother's life. Having left for England in 1603 to rule the kingdom he called Great Britain, James returned to Scotland only once, in 1617.

QUEEN AND SON

Mary Queen of Scots with her son James VI. James was just a year old when Mary abdicated. She never saw him again, so the painting is an imaginary sitting of them together.

EXECUTION OF MARY

A Dutch drawing published about 1608 shows the scene at Fotheringhay Castle as the executioner prepares to strike off Mary's head. Her clothes and the block were burned (shown on the left) to leave no relics for veneration.

STUARTS AND
HOUSE OF ORANGE

HOUSES OF STUART AND ORANGE

James I
(**James VI** of Scotland)
1603–1625 = Anne of Denmark

Henry Frederick   **Charles I** 1625–1649 = Henrietta Maria   Elizabeth = Frederick V Elector Palatine

Mary = William Prince of Orange   **James II** 1685–1688 = Anne Hyde (1st wife) = Mary of Modena (2nd wife)   **Charles II** 1660–1685 = Catherine of Braganza

William III 1689–1702 = **Mary II** 1689–1694   **Anne** 1702–1714 = George of Denmark

James Francis Edward (the 'Old Pretender') = Maria Clementina Sobieska

Charles Edward (Bonnie Prince Charlie)   Henry Benedict Cardinal

Sophia = Ernest Augustus Elector of Hanover

George I 1714–1727

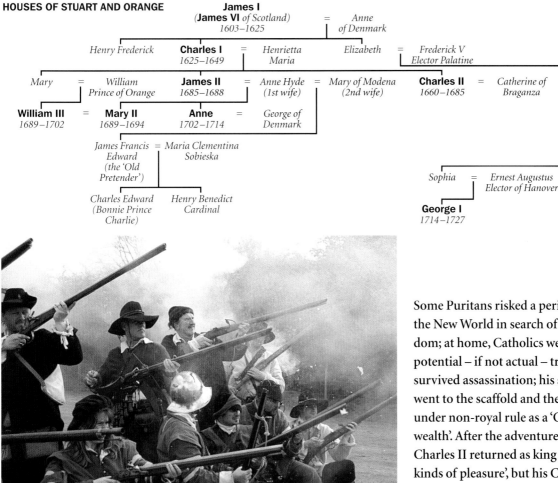

CIVIL WAR SMOKE AND FURY

A re-enacted musket volley. Loading and firing Civil War handguns was laborious, but musket balls caused heavy casualties.

THE QUEEN'S HOUSE AT GREENWICH

In 1616, Inigo Jones planned a Palladian-style house for Queen Anne, wife of James I, on the site of the old Tudor palace at Greenwich. The Queen's House was not completed until 1635, for Charles I's queen, Henrietta Maria.

IN 1603, ENGLAND WAS READY to welcome its first Scottish monarch, and James I was equally ready to embrace London's pleasures after the dourness of Calvinist Scotland. The union of Crowns promised a new and greater Britain. Yet under the Stuarts, England – and to a lesser extent Scotland – was almost torn apart by religious and political division. The Jacobean age (from *Jacobus*, Latin for James) was a darker, more questioning time than the era of Tudor optimism.

Some Puritans risked a perilous voyage to the New World in search of religious freedom; at home, Catholics were seen as potential – if not actual – traitors. James I survived assassination; his son Charles I went to the scaffold and the nation came under non-royal rule as a 'Commonwealth'. After the adventures of exile, Charles II returned as king to enjoy 'all kinds of pleasure', but his Catholic brother James II was forced out of the country in 1688. And so the Crown passed to James's daughter, Mary, and her Dutch husband, William of Orange, and subsequently to Queen Anne, last of the Stuarts.

The 17th century saw the Civil War won by Cromwell and his Ironsides, the Great Plague in 1665 and Great Fire of London the following year. It produced the true-life epic of the *Mayflower* pilgrims, and John Milton's poetic epic *Paradise Lost*. It was lit by the careers of Christopher Wren and Isaac Newton, and diverted by innovations such as telescopes and tea-drinking. When Queen Anne died in 1714, her German cousin George of Hanover arrived to take the Crown, though the exiled Stuarts still had cards to play.

James I (1603–25)

James – son of Henry Stuart, Lord Darnley, and Mary Queen of Scots – became King James VI of Scotland in 1567, the year after his birth. He then waited patiently for Elizabeth I to die, when the thrones of England and Scotland might be joined, and in 1589 married Anne of Denmark. The couple had seven children.

James was greeted with enthusiasm in 1603 when he rode south. A popular king of Scotland, he loved England, but the English were soon less sure about him. Physically awkward, spluttering in speech and slobbering over his food, James was intelligent, but a

James VI becomes James I

James's claim to the English throne came from his great-grandmother Margaret (died 1541), sister of Henry VIII. Elizabeth had accepted him as her heir.

Classical masterpiece

The Banqueting House in Whitehall, built for James I by Inigo Jones, 1619–22, was the first great Classical-style building in England. Charles I was beheaded outside it in 1649.

A RELIEVED ROYAL ADDRESS

James speaking to Parliament after the discovery of the Gunpowder
Plot, as the plotters are arrested below. The House of Lords' cellars are
still ceremoniously searched before the State Opening of Parliament.

bundle of phobias. His behaviour with courtiers was effu-
sively homosexual, and his favourites – notably Robert
Carr, Earl of Somerset, and George Villiers, Duke of
Buckingham – were disliked by many.

James had strong opinions – the French ambassador
called him 'the wisest fool in Christendom'. He believed in
the Divine Right of Kings (that consecrated kings are the
direct representatives of God) and in bishops: 'no Bishop,
no King,' he had lectured Scots Calvinists. He detested
tobacco smoking and feared witchcraft, but is best
remembered for lending his regal stamp to the
Authorized (King James's) Version of the Bible – and
for not being blown up by Guy Fawkes.

In England, James was treated with more grandeur than
in Scotland, but power was increasingly shared between
king and Parliament. Failure to step delicately around this
constitutional pitfall was to prove fatal for James's son
and successor, Charles I.

GUNPOWDER, TREASON AND PLOT …

In May 1604, five Catholic plotters met at the
Duck and Drake tavern in London. Even by
modern terrorist standards, gang leader Robert
Catesby's plan was spectacular – to blow up
the Houses of Parliament with the king and his
lords inside them. Though most of the plotters
were amateurs, Guido (Guy) Fawkes was a
professional soldier. James I had failed to relax
anti-Catholic laws, so they hoped to replace
him (and his sons) with his daughter, Princess
Elizabeth, who at nine years old could be raised
as a Catholic and marry another.

Catesby was being watched, and aroused
suspicion by casual recruiting of new plotters.
Then an anonymous letter to Lord Mounteagle,
a Catholic lord, warned him not to attend the
Opening of Parliament. The letter went to
Sir Robert Cecil, James's chief minister.

On the morning of 5 November 1605, Guy
Fawkes was caught in the vaults beneath the
House of Lords with 36 barrels of gunpowder.
The other plotters fled, but were either killed
resisting arrest or brought to London for torture
and death. The gunpowder proved to have
decayed; even if lit, it may not have exploded.

'Now surely in my opinion, there cannot
be a more base and hurtful corruption in
our country than is the vile use of taking
Tobacco in this Kingdom.'

A Counterblast to Tobacco, James I, 1604

CHARLES I (1625–49)

HENRIETTA MARIA
Charles was a fond husband and father. His queen had five children: two sons (later Charles II and James II) and three daughters, of whom the eldest (Mary) was to be mother of William III.

CHARLES ON HORSEBACK
The court painter Sir Anthony Van Dyck shows a confident yet sensitive king, ruling a land at peace. This was how Charles I wistfully wanted his subjects to see him.

JAMES I'S ELDEST SON, Prince Henry, died in 1612, leaving his brother Charles as heir to the throne. Slightly built, with a hesitation in his speech, Charles grew to be reserved yet courteous, interested in the arts, and a lover of horses and hunting. He proved a dutiful husband to Henrietta Maria, the French wife he married soon after becoming king on 27 March 1625.

Charles shied away from extremes in religious matters. Nor had he any wish to haggle with Parliament over money, putting his trust in strong counsellors: the Duke of Buckingham; Thomas Wentworth, Earl of Strafford; Archbishop Laud. But Charles's foreign policy went badly wrong: expensive wars with France and Spain had disastrous results.

Parliament refused to vote more taxes, Buckingham was assassinated in 1629, and the Scots 'Covenanters' went to war with their own king. Infuriated, Charles dismissed the 'Short Parliament' but was forced to call another (the 'Long Parliament') in 1640. The Commons turned on Strafford, charging the king's minister with treason, and Charles had to condemn his loyal servant to death. Growing in confidence, Parliament then demanded that Charles give up command of the army. 'By God, not for an hour,' the king retorted.

So a mild monarch was sucked into civil war. Charles had few allies in Parliament, or London, and his clumsy attempts at strong leadership – for example, by arresting Members of Parliament – backfired badly. When in 1642 the king raised his standard to fight, he was in Nottingham. London was Parliament's.

For seven years of war, Charles showed personal courage, but no real strategy. Captured in 1647, he might have escaped to France but instead ended in prison on the Isle of Wight. Then, rather than try for a compromise settlement, he tried to 'divide and rule', again pinning his hopes on the Scots, who handed him over to Parliament. Tried in Westminster Hall 'as a tyrant and a traitor', Charles faced his accusers with calm dignity. Sentenced to death, he was beheaded outside the Banqueting House in Whitehall. To the end he remained dismissive of Parliament's right to try him: 'a king cannot be tried by any superior jurisdiction on earth'.

THE BIRDS HAVE FLOWN!

Confrontation in the House of Commons (4 January 1642) when Charles demanded the surrender of five MPs he considered rebel ringleaders. The five had slipped away; and both sides realized that war must follow.

'Truly I desire [the people's] liberty and freedom as much as anybody whomsoever.'

Charles I, speaking shortly before his execution

DEATH OF A KING

Philip Henry, an undergraduate at Oxford, saw the execution of Charles I, on Tuesday 30 January 1649. 'I stood among the crowd in the street before Whitehall gate where the scaffold was erected, and saw what was done … The blow I saw given, and can truly say with a sad heart, at the instant whereof,

I remember well, there was such a groan by the thousands there present as I never heard before and desire I may never hear again.'

THE CIVIL WAR AND THE COMMONWEALTH: 1642–60

THE CIVIL WAR that began in England spread to engulf Scotland, Ireland and Wales. Men and women at all levels of society – even within the same family – took different sides on issues of principle. The struggle between king and Parliament was heightened by religious differences between Puritans and Anglicans, and by calls for social equality or 'levelling' from small groups of radicals.

The war began in 1642 when Charles raised his standard at Nottingham – only for it to be blown down the same night 'by a very strong and unruly wind'. This was a bad omen. The first major battle – at Edgehill, Warwickshire (on 23 October 1642) – was indecisive. Prominent among Parliament's ranks was Oliver Cromwell, a 43-year-old gentleman-farmer from the Fens who reformed his side's cavalry to a point where it matched the dash of the king's cavaliers, commanded by his nephew, Prince Rupert.

In a war of frequent, mainly small, battles there were seldom more than 15,000 men on either side. Of some 645 actions recorded, 198 were sieges, averaging a

THE BATTLE OF DUNBAR

Cromwell wrote to the Speaker of Parliament after the Battle of Dunbar, 1650: 'The enemy made a gallant resistance, and there was a very hot dispute at sword's point between our horse and theirs'. He goes on to describe how his own regiment 'at the push of pike, did repel the stoutest regiment the enemy had, merely with the courage the Lord was pleased to give ...' The battle ended with a rout **'our men having the chase and execution of them near eight miles.'**

THE BATTLE OF MARSTON MOOR

Marston Moor, the bloodiest Civil War battle, was fought near York in the summer of 1644. 'God made them as stubble to our swords,' declared Cromwell, whose cavalry won the day.

month or more. Some castles and churches suffered severe damage and there was human cost, too. Between 1642 and 1660, over 84,000 people were killed. Disease took perhaps 150,000 more lives. Ireland lost as much as 40 per cent of its population.

King Charles's hopes of clear victory were dashed by defeat at Naseby in 1645. He then tried diplomatic manoeuvres, but in the end was brought to trial and execution. Hopes of a Royalist counterstroke from Ireland were crushed by Cromwell, and the Royalists' defeat at Worcester in 1651 ended the war as Charles II escaped to exile abroad.

Kingless England was declared a Commonwealth. In 1653, however, Cromwell tired of a bickering Parliament and ironically ruled alone as Lord Protector, refusing the title of king in 1657. When Cromwell died in 1658, his son Richard, mockingly nicknamed 'Tumbledown Dick', inherited his father's position but quickly resigned. To general relief, the army and Parliament invited Charles II to return from exile.

A BRAVE DEATH

Ernest Croft's Victorian painting shows Charles I on the scaffold. On a bitterly cold winter's morning, the king wore two shirts to avoid shivering and so appear fearful of impending death.

PROTECTOR OF PARLIAMENT?

Today this statue of Oliver Cromwell stands outside the Houses of Parliament, whose rights and privileges he fought to defend but whose services he later dispensed with.

'For my part, I began to think we should all, like Abraham, live in tents all the days of our lives …'

Lady Anne Fanshawe (1625–80), on life during the Civil War

OLIVER
CROMWELL
1599
1658

KEY EVENTS IN THE CIVIL WAR

1642	Civil War begins. Battle of Edgehill
1644	Battle of Marston Moor
1645	Parliament's New Model Army wins Battle of Naseby
1646	Charles I surrenders to Scots
1647	Scots hand Charles to the Army, but he escapes
1648	Charles allies himself with Scots; second stage of war begins
1649	Trial and execution of Charles I
1651	Charles II is defeated at Worcester
1653	Cromwell becomes Lord Protector
1658	Death of Cromwell
1660	Monarchy is restored

CHARLES II AND JAMES II: 1660–88

CHARLES II (1660–85)

CHARLES GREW TO BE taller than most, dark-complexioned with sparkling eyes and a mass of curly hair. Just 12 when the Civil War began, his adventures as a fugitive after the Battle of Worcester (1651) passed into folklore. Restored to the throne in 1660, he returned from exile to a triumphant coronation and, on the whole, the Restoration was tolerant, with no great persecution of Cromwell's supporters. In 1662, the king married Catherine of Braganza, a Portuguese princess. There were no children of the marriage, but Charles had plenty of illegitimate offspring by his many mistresses.

'He is so ugly I am ashamed … but his size and fatness supply what he lacks in beauty.'

Queen Henrietta Maria, on her two-year-old son Charles, later Charles II

'AN EXACT KNOWER OF MANKIND'

This was one description of Charles II. In this regal portrait, some may see the cynicism that such knowledge imparted.

THE MERRY MONARCH TAKES THE FLOOR

Charles II dances with Mary of Orange (his sister) at a ball in Holland on the eve of the Restoration.

SOUVENIR MUG

Charles II features on this cup, made at the Restoration. Charles popularized yacht racing, skating and horse racing in England.

Most capable of all the English Stuarts, Charles was astute enough to avoid political pitfalls, while enjoying court life to the full. He liked dogs, horse racing, yachts and actresses, but was also interested in science – the Greenwich Observatory and Royal Society were founded during his reign. Though Samuel Pepys might tut-tut over the 'sad, vicious and negligent Court', the Merry Monarch's reign saw the nation survive two major disasters: the Great Plague of 1665, in which more than 100,000 people died, and the Great Fire of London in 1666, which destroyed 13,000 homes in the city but miraculously killed not a single person.

Before he died, Charles was quietly accepted into the Roman Catholic faith. His brother James's more aggressive Catholicism plunged the country back into crisis.

JAMES II (1685–88)

Three years younger than his brother, James had escaped to Holland during the Civil War in 1648, dressed as a girl. A brave soldier who served with the French and Spanish armies, he was given command of the English navy by King Charles II.

Bravery was not enough, for 'Dismal Jimmy' was humourless and stubborn to a fault. His first marriage, to Anne Hyde, produced two daughters – Mary and Anne – who were raised as Protestants though James became openly Catholic. His second marriage (1673) to the Catholic princess Mary of Modena was unpopular and Parliament tried to bar James from the throne.

Soon after he became king in 1685, rebellions by the Duke of Argyll in Scotland and in England by the Duke of Monmouth (son of Charles II) fizzled out; the repression that followed was counter-productive.

Fears of a new Catholic dynasty were raised by the birth in June 1688 of a son to James's queen. Messages went to the king's Protestant son-in-law, William of Orange, offering him the throne and William duly landed with an army on 15 November. James hurriedly sent his wife and son abroad. After a futile attempt to bargain, he fled but was caught, returned to London and was then allowed to sail for France. In 1689, James landed with an army in Ireland, but his hopes ended in defeat at the Battle of the Boyne (1 July 1690). He died in exile in 1701.

JAMES IN EXILE

Painted in France after James II's humiliating departure from England, this portrait shows a man who knows he has thrown away a kingdom.

'He was perpetually in one amour or the other, without being very nice in his choice.'

Gilbert Burnet, Bishop of Salisbury, on James II

THE GREAT FIRE

2 September 1666. 'Jane called us up about three in the morning, to tell us of a great fire they saw in the City …'. Thus the diarist Samuel Pepys first learned of the Great Fire of London. The day was one of confusion, people rushing to fling their belongings into boats on the Thames, or staying in their houses until the last minute before fleeing. Pepys ended the day in a little alehouse, from where ' **... it being darkish, we saw the fire as only one entire arch of fire from this to the other side of the bridge** [London Bridge],' and he wept to see 'the churches, houses, and all on fire.'

WILLIAM AND MARY, AND ANNE: 1689–1714

WILLIAM III (1689–1702) AND MARY II (1689–94)

WILLIAM OF ORANGE WAS the son of William II, Prince of Orange, and Mary, daughter of Charles I. Though stooped and asthmatic, the Dutch ruler was tough and shrewd, trained from boyhood for state affairs. Lively as a young man, he grew more stiffly reserved with age but was fond of his wife Mary, the young cousin he had married in 1677 when she was only 15. Mary, daughter of James II and Anne Hyde, had wept bitterly at the prospect of marrying a Dutchman she had never met, but performed her royal duty placidly. She was a gentle soul, given to good works and liked by all.

'He spoke little and very slowly … except in a day of battle, for then he was all fire … he was everywhere and looked to everything.'

Gilbert Burnet, Bishop of Salisbury, on William III

William and Mary's arrival in 1688 as joint monarchs was confirmed by Convention Parliaments in England and Scotland – in other words, the monarchy had now become a Parliamentary institution. Apart from isolated protests (in Scotland, the Glencoe massacre of 1692 was a punishment for Macdonald slowness in swearing allegiance to the new king), the transition was peaceful – a 'Glorious Revolution' in the eyes of its supporters.

William's mission was in mainland Europe, where as champion of 'small-nation Protestantism' he worked to sustain a coalition against Louis XIV of France, and had led armies with some success. Popular among the ordinary English, the taciturn king was disliked by most of the nobility.

When Mary died from smallpox in 1694, William was distressed – 'you know what it is to have a good wife,' he told a friend. The couple were childless and, with no idea of remarrying, the king planned to make Mary's sister Anne his heir (the Act of Settlement in 1701 stipulating that future monarchs must be Protestant). He also planned to send the Duke of Marlborough as commander of the coalition army against the French. William died after an accident at Hampton Court; his horse caught its hoof in a molehill, the king fell, and he died on 19 March 1702. James II's supporters afterwards toasted the 'velvet-coated gentleman' [the mole].

RECEIVING THE CROWN

William and Mary are presented with the crown; new crown jewels had been made for Charles II as most of the old ones were destroyed during the Commonwealth.

ANNE (1702–14)

Anne duly inherited the throne at the age of 36. Resolutely ordinary, she was a devout Anglican who favoured the Tory party (more monarchical) above the Whigs (inclined towards the aristocracy as a balance to royal power). The queen's best friend was Sarah Jennings, wife of John Churchill – first Duke of Marlborough and England's most brilliant general – whose victories at Blenheim, Oudenarde, Ramillies and Malplaquet were hailed with patriotic fervour.

Anne's marriage to Prince George of Denmark (of whom Charles II had remarked, 'I have tried him drunk and tried him sober, but there is nothing in him either way,') produced 17 children who all died in infancy or early childhood. The main event of her reign was the union of England and Scotland under one Parliament in 1707.

MESSAGE FROM MARLBOROUGH

The Duke of Marlborough signs a despatch to his wife Sarah with news of his victory at the Battle of Blenheim in 1704.

QUEEN ANNE BY KNELLER

Sir Godfrey Kneller's portrait of Anne shows her in robes of state. The queen suffered almost constant ill-health; her favourite pastimes were cards, tea parties and admiring gardens.

' … *a clear harmonious voice, particularly conspicuous in her graceful delivery of her speeches to Parliament.*'

History of the Life and Reign of Queen Anne, *Abel Boyer, 1702*

ROYAL PALACES

A HOUSE FIT FOR
A QUEEN

*The Queen's House at
Greenwich was built in an
H-shape, astride the Deptford to
Woolwich road. On either side
now stand the galleries of the
National Maritime Museum,
originally the naval equivalent
of the Royal Hospital, Chelsea.*

THE STUARTS WERE KEEN PATRONS of the arts. James I asked Inigo Jones to create the elegant Queen's House at Greenwich and the Banqueting House at Whitehall Palace. Jones, who made his name as a set designer for elaborate theatrical masques, had introduced to England the Palladian neoclassical style of architecture.

Work at Greenwich began in 1616 but halted when Anne, James I's queen, fell ill (she died in 1619). Building continued in 1629, and Charles I gave the house to his wife Henrietta Maria. Leading painters from Europe were imported to decorate the interior. Charles' favourite painter was Van Dyck, but to paint the Banqueting House ceiling he engaged Rubens. Another Flemish artist, Peter Lely, was hired to paint portraits of the king and ladies of the court, and the Italian Anthony Verrio to decorate Windsor Castle.

Charles II's most inspired move was to appoint Christopher Wren as Surveyor General. When, after London's Great Fire, Wren rebuilt St Paul's Cathedral and 52 other London churches, he became the royal architect of choice. William and Mary disliked Whitehall Palace (sprawlingly medieval and – being so near the Thames – damp and unhealthy) and so asked Wren to create a new palace at Kensington, where William had bought a mansion named Nottingham House. Wren enlarged this in five months of frantic work, in time for Christmas 1689. Additions in the 1690s included the Queen's Staircase and King's Gallery, while a charming Orangery was added in 1704, during Queen Anne's reign.

KENSINGTON PALACE

William and Mary's choice of home, a suburban mansion, was transformed into a modest palace on rising ground in its own gardens.

Most of Whitehall Palace burned down in 1698, when a laundry room caught fire. St James's Palace then became a principal London royal residence, with rooms added by Wren for James II joining the sovereign's state suite.

When William and Mary asked Wren to extend Hampton Court's old Tudor palace, he produced the Fountain Court, and around it the splendid King's Apartments (restored after fire damage in 1986). Work on the Queen's State Apartments stopped when Mary died but Queen Anne commissioned further work, although the apartments were not finished until the reign of George II – the last king to live in Hampton Court Palace. Keen gardeners, William and Mary redesigned Hampton Court's gardens, originally laid out for Henry VIII. The Privy Garden and famous maze date from 1702, while the Lower Orangery was built for Queen Mary's collection of exotic plants.

MASTER ARCHITECT

Johann Closterman's portrait of Sir Christopher Wren as President of the Royal Society, c. 1683. St Paul's Cathedral is shown in the background.

There are few royal buildings to rival the Royal Pavilion at Brighton, John Nash's extravagant transformation (1815–22) of a Sussex farmhouse into a fantasy of pleasure domes for the Prince Regent, later George IV.

COLLAPSE OF STUART HOPES

At the Battle of Culloden in 1746, Bonnie Prince Charlie's Highland army, brave but ill-equipped, was slaughtered by cannon and musket fire from Cumberland's redcoats. The Hanoverian succession was secure.

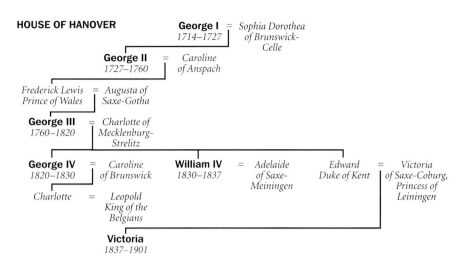

HOUSE OF HANOVER

George I 1714–1727	=	*Sophia Dorothea of Brunswick-Celle*
George II 1727–1760	=	*Caroline of Anspach*
Frederick Lewis Prince of Wales	=	*Augusta of Saxe-Gotha*
George III 1760–1820	=	*Charlotte of Mecklenburg-Strelitz*

George IV 1820–1830	=	*Caroline of Brunswick*	**William IV** 1830–1837	=	*Adelaide of Saxe-Meiningen*	*Edward Duke of Kent*	=	*Victoria of Saxe-Coburg, Princess of Leiningen*

Charlotte	=	*Leopold King of the Belgians*

Victoria 1837–1901

But there were striking contrasts. Learned societies flourished while schools and universities stagnated. Elegant mansions ornamented the countryside while towns seethed and stank.

The Hanoverian kings – George I to William IV – survived Jacobite rebellions, American and French revolutions,

THE 18TH CENTURY SAW Britain's first three King Georges: 'German George', 'Soldier George' and 'Farmer George'. Although known as the Age of Reason, this period of history was often both irrational and emotional. The term 'Georgian' – whether applied to architecture, fashion or poetry – might suggest a culture of calm order, but in fact society was a bubbling, unstable mixture stirred by ideas of the day: classical formality, romantic naturalism, rational science and political idealism.

Georgian Britons – at least of the upper classes – were prosperous, sturdily self-sufficient, argumentative and optimistic. They lived through political upheavals and the early phases of farming and industrial revolutions that were to transform their land and their lives.

foreign wars and the birth of 'party politics'. It was an age of achievement in many fields – in literature, art and architecture, science and exploration, as well as military success, particularly at sea. Britannia was indeed beginning to rule the waves.

By the time George IV and his brother William brought the Hanoverian dynasty to a rather ragged end, Britain had risen victorious from a long war with Napoleon's France. The nation was now a world power, proud of its liberties, confident in its wealth, with the foundations laid for overseas empire and industrial dominance. The Hanoverian kings may have been much mocked by cartoonists, but they had reigned over a largely fortunate era.

GEORGE I AND GEORGE II: 1714–60

GEORGE I (1714–27)

THE 1701 ACT OF SETTLEMENT declared that Queen Anne's heir should be Sophia, Electress of Hanover and grand-daughter of James I. When first Sophia, and then Queen Anne, died in 1714, Sophia's son George Lewis (born in 1660) became King of Great Britain. The change of dynasty passed surprisingly peacefully and George arrived in his new kingdom a month later.

'I hate all boets and bainters.' Attributed to George I – his views on the arts

Although a German who spoke to his ministers in French, George was Protestant – a condition of the Act of Settlement. Fair, with froglike eyes, and saying little in any language, he left government to politicians – a crucial constitutional development, for George's most trusted minister, Sir Robert Walpole, became the country's first 'Prime Minister'. A pro-Stuart rebellion in Scotland was put down in 1715, while in 1720 came a financial crisis – the crash of the South Sea Bubble.

HAVE YOU HEARD THIS ONE, BISHOP?

Sir Robert Walpole and his Cabinet – the shocked expression of the bishop (right) suggests that the wily First Lord of the Treasury might be telling one of the bawdy stories for which he was notorious.

94

'That is one big lie.' George II, on hearing from Walpole that his father was dead

George's personal life was less than admirable – he divorced and locked up his wife Sophia Dorothea, kept two German mistresses and quarrelled with his son. Yet he liked music, brought Handel to England and displayed interest in agricultural 'improvements' – asking, for example, whether it would be economical to plant St James's Park with turnips. Much preferring Hanover to London, he died on the way to Germany in 1727, having been taken ill in his coach.

GEORGE II (1727–60)

George II has been called many names – self-important, fussy, hardworking, skirt-chasing – and gave rise to many stories. Thirty when his father arrived in England in 1714, the prince and his wife – beautiful, intelligent and flirtatious Caroline of Anspach – set up a rival court where cards and dancing were enjoyed out of the king's sight. Tall, with blue eyes and a ruddy face, George II loved military uniforms as much as he despised his father (who had, after all, locked up his mother).

A time of peace and prosperity, George II's reign was the heyday of the English aristocracy, whose great houses and parks studded the land. George made friends with the owners, declaring stoutly: 'I have not one drop of blood in my veins that is not English.' Wily Prime Minister Walpole knew the way to the king was through the queen, commenting that he had 'the right sow by the ear'.

GEORGE THE GENERAL

George II on horseback, with his army in the background. His victory over the French at Dettingen in Bavaria (27 June 1743) was the last battle in which a reigning British monarch took part.

Gaining the throne at the age of 44, George II – a brave man – was the last king to lead British troops into battle, at Dettingen in 1743. Two years later, the Hanoverian monarchy survived the Jacobite rebellion of 1745.

Heartbroken when Queen Caroline died in 1737, the king grieved less at the death of his son 'Fred' in 1751, for the two quarrelled violently whenever they met. George reigned on alone, dying (in the lavatory) in 1760, of a heart attack.

95

BONNIE PRINCE CHARLIE

'I wash my hands of the fatal consequences which I foresee but cannot help.'

Bonnie Prince Charlie, shortly before the Battle of Culloden

THE BONNIE PRINCE

This portrait by Louis-Gabriel Blanchet shows Charles Edward Stuart as the elegant prince who was to charm his way into Scottish legend.

IN 1745, PRINCE CHARLES EDWARD STUART began his ill-fated attempt to reclaim the throne lost by his grandfather in 1688.

When James II died in exile in 1701, his son James Francis Edward was proclaimed King James III in France. His supporters were known as Jacobites, after the Latin *Jacobus* (James). James, the 'Old Pretender', made a failed bid for his father's crown in 1715, after which Scottish Jacobites gave their loyalty to James's son, Charles Edward Louis Philip Casimir Stuart. Born in Rome in 1720 to the Polish princess Maria Clementina Sobieska, he is remembered in history as 'Bonnie Prince Charlie' of the '45.

Convinced that Scotland and then England would rally to him, Charles landed in the Hebrides on 23 July 1745. A predicted rapturous welcome from Highland clans was wide of the mark, but eventually some 1,200 men gathered around his standard to proclaim James king and Charles his regent.

The 'Young Pretender' entered Edinburgh a month later with 2,500 infantry and 50 horses, winning the Battle of Prestonpans on 21 September. Gracious in victory – 'Spare them, they are my father's subjects,' he ordered – Charles prevented a general slaughter. His intention was to attack Newcastle and then march on to London, but Lord George Murray instead insisted

THE BATTLE OF CULLODEN

In this painting by David Morier, government redcoats with fixed bayonets stand firm against the Highlanders' charge: the battle was to last only 25 minutes.

FLORA MACDONALD

Born in 1722, Flora was arrested after Charles's escape, and briefly held in the Tower of London. Released in 1747, she married and emigrated to America in 1774. After returning to Scotland, she died in 1790.

LOCHABER NO MORE

In J.B. Macdonald's painting, Charles takes leave of Scotland in September 1746, his ambition to be king dashed forever.

PRINCE IN DISGUISE

After Culloden, Charles lived as a fugitive in the heather. In August 1746, greeted by a loyal Jacobite, he hastily stopped the man from kneeling in homage with the wry warning: **'Oh no, my dear Lochiel, you don't know who may be looking from the tops of yonder hills.'** Three weeks later, he was gone forever.

on caution. Pipes skirling, the Highlanders marched into Carlisle on 1 November. By 28 November Charles was in Manchester, and on 4 December in Derby.

In London, panic began; shops closed as King George II was rumoured to be leaving for Hanover. Yet at this point the Scots advance stopped. Murray was alarmed at the dearth of English support, Charles was outvoted, and on 6 December the retreat began – with the Duke of Cumberland's English army in pursuit.

Six thousand weary, hungry Highlanders gathered on Inverness-shire's bleak Culloden Moor on 16 April 1746. Cumberland had 9,000 troops, rested and fed, along with artillery. The battle was soon over, leaving the ground piled with dead clansmen. Those wounded were butchered or left to die, their bodies rotting on the moor.

'Let every man seek his safety in the best way that he can,' Charles ordered, and for five months he wandered the Western highlands – his fugitive adventures remembered in such tales as being disguised by Flora Macdonald as 'Betty Burke', a servant girl. An open boat took him 'over the sea to Skye' and on 20 September 1746 he left Scotland, never to return.

The Highlands endured privation and misery while Charles lived out his years in exile. He left no heir. At his death in Rome in 1788, his brother Henry (a cardinal) called himself Henry IX and was awarded a pension by the kindly George III. On Henry's death in 1807, the direct male Stuart line died out.

GEORGE III (1760–1820)

WHEN FREDERICK, PRINCE OF WALES died in 1751 his 12-year-old son became the next heir to the throne and was duly crowned George III. Unlike his grandfather, George was thoroughly English, and proud of it. An example of domestic virtue and conscientious to a fault, he 'gloried in the name of Briton'.

In 1761 George married a German princess, Charlotte of Mecklenburg-Strelitz, and their happy union produced 15 children. Simple in his tastes, the king loved farming and craftsmanship; he found politics a hard world to fathom, offering little in the way of true friendship. The ministers that he trusted – Bute and North – proved to be broken reeds, but George shrewdly saw that an untried, somewhat uncongenial politician (William Pitt the Younger, Prime Minister at only 24) could provide more reliable support. Pitt led the government for 21 years, through tumultuous times.

THE MADNESS OF KING GEORGE

George's illness first appeared when he had convulsions, and seemed unable to stop talking. One famous story – but unproven – has the king speaking to an oak tree in the belief that it was the King of Prussia. His illness took a serious turn in November 1788 when he attacked the Prince of Wales over the Windsor Castle dinner table. A brief recovery was greeted with popular relief; the king went bathing in the sea at Weymouth as a band on the beach played **'God Save the King'**.

FARMER GEORGE IN STATE
George III was hard-working and well-meaning, though his enemies unfairly tried to portray him as a would-be despot.

George III was a passionate opponent of Napoleon Bonaparte and, with the nation, hailed the navy's victory at Trafalgar in October 1805 while mourning the death of Admiral Nelson. **'England has saved herself by her exertions and will, I trust, save Europe by its example,'** declared Prime Minister William Pitt a month later.

A NEW FAMILY HOME

In 1762 George III left Kensington Palace (where his father's ghost was said to appear) for a new home, Buckingham House. There he and Queen Charlotte planned 'sumptuous and stately improvements' to what became Buckingham Palace.

George III's was a reign of political upheaval, at home and abroad. The king had to cope with fallout from the American and French Revolutions, and losing the American colonies in 1783 was a severe blow for which George himself was widely, though unfairly, blamed. But when war with revolutionary France broke out in 1793, the king became a symbol of patriotic resistance to tyranny and anarchy – making the monarchy more popular than it had been since the days of Charles II.

A LOVING WIFE

Queen Charlotte proved a loving and dutiful wife to 'Farmer George', who wrote pamphlets on farming under the pseudonym 'Ralph Robinson'.

From middle age, George had bouts of illness affecting him mentally and physically. He suffered from porphyria, a genetic condition that in the 18th century was treated as 'lunacy' with remedies often more distressing than the sickness. From 1810 he was permanently disabled, ending his life a sad and confused old man in a dressing gown, wandering around Windsor Castle. When 'Farmer George' died in January 1820 his merits soon became clear – in contrast with his son and successor, George IV.

GEORGE IV AND WILLIAM IV: 1821–37

GEORGE IV

Flamboyant George loved dressing up. He admired Jane Austen but almost sold his father's books (now in the British Library) to the Tsar.

GEORGE IV (1821–30)

BORN IN 1762, GEORGE IV understudied the sovereign's role as Prince Regent during his father's illness. During this time, wayward 'Prinny' did his utmost to destroy the respect painstakingly earned by George III.

Artistic, imaginative, handsome, the Prince was charming to women (who cooed over 'the irresistible sweetness of his smile, the tenderness of his melodious yet manly voice'). But over-eating and drinking soon transformed George into the cartoonists' gross 'Voluptuary under the horrors of Digestion' – apoplectic and almost bursting out of his breeches.

The love of his life was Mrs Maria Fitzherbert, a Catholic widow he married in secret. His 'official' marriage in 1795 to a German cousin, Caroline of Brunswick, proved short: 'I am not well, pray get me a glass of brandy,' were his words when they met. The couple separated after a daughter, Charlotte, was born in 1796. Arriving for the coronation in 1821, the queen was shut out of Westminster Abbey.

George liked fashionable clothes and company, such as George (Beau) Brummel. He made Brighton and Bath the places to see and be seen. As king, George IV forsook the radical views he had spouted to annoy his father, playing no part in the reign's reforms (of criminal law and police; free trade; more religious freedoms for Catholics and Nonconformists). Princess Charlotte having died in childbirth in 1817, George IV was succeeded by his brother, William.

WILLIAM IV (1830–37)

'Silly Billy' was George III's third son, born in 1765. Nobody expected him to become king and so he was sent into the navy – hence his more flattering nickname, 'The Sailor King'.

THE ROYAL PAVILION, BRIGHTON

The domes, pinnacles and minarets of Brighton's Royal Pavilion make it Britain's most exotic royal palace. In 1786 – a year after marrying Mrs Fitzherbert – the Prince of Wales took a modest farmhouse, transformed between 1815–22 by John Nash into an oriental fantasy palace with Chinese interiors and a dramatic Banqueting Room. The Pavilion is a unique memorial to Regency taste, extravagantly indulged.

Cheery and excitable, William lived in cosy, unmarried bliss with the actress Dorothea Jordan and their ten children, but – pressured by the royal family – in 1818 he married Princess Adelaide of Saxe-Meiningen. The deaths of Princess Charlotte and his older brother, the Duke of York, made him next in line to the throne.

William was thrilled to be king, riding about London in a carriage, waving to passers-by. His modest coronation was in marked contrast to George IV's and his

'Who is Silly Billy now?'
William IV, speaking to his Privy Council

acceptance of the 1832 Reform Act – though reluctant – showed the monarchy adjusting to a world in which 'One man, one vote' became a clarion call.

Good-hearted, and showing unexpected common sense in a crisis, William had no surviving children from his marriage to Queen Adelaide. It was his niece, Princess Victoria, who succeeded 'Silly Billy' in June 1837.

THE SAILOR KING

William IV spent his early years at sea, and served under Nelson in the West Indies. He fretted over the fact that he had never been given his own command.

101

WINDSOR CASTLE

WINDSOR CASTLE REMAINS THE largest castle still used as a residence. Parts date from the early Norman Conquest, when William I put up a wooden castle around 1070. Henry II built the great round tower in 1180, and Edward III made the Chapel of St George the centre of his new Order of the Garter in 1348.

Later monarchs – including Henry VIII, Elizabeth I and Charles I – made various changes. The Long Walk, planted by Charles II in 1685, had 1,650 elm trees (replaced in 1945 by plane and chestnut). George IV transformed the austere medieval castle into a comfortable royal residence. Royal Lodge in the park was one of his favourite retreats.

Queen Victoria found Windsor more relaxingly rural than London's Buckingham Palace. It was also more accessible by the new railway. The young queen spent her honeymoon at Windsor, and the castle became the scene of royal family Christmas festivities. Among other alterations, new drains were installed in the 1840s though these failed to prevent the death of Prince Albert who in 1861 contracted typhoid – probably from the castle's inadequate sewers.

Security today is somewhat tighter than in Victoria's time, when people wandered freely around the park and castle. In 1849 some light-fingered visitors stole a royal sketchbook, publishing its contents for sale.

ESCAPE FROM THE FLAMES

The 1992 fire is commemorated in this stained-glass window, showing paintings being rescued from the flames. Fortunately, few treasures were lost.

ITALIAN-STYLE GARDEN

The formal garden, beneath the East Front of the castle, has the appearance of a sunken garden and was created for George IV.

HONEYMOON SUITE

Victoria and Albert honeymooned at Windsor, driving out from London in a carriage with an escort of well-wishers. They explored the royal suite together, and Albert tried out the piano. The young queen was then stricken with a headache and collapsed on the sofa as 'My dearest, dearest, dear Albert sat on a footstool by my side'.

The castle is the resting place for many monarchs and their consorts. The memorial chapel, designed by Henry VII as a mausoleum, was restored at Victoria's wish as the Albert Memorial Chapel and is the burial place of George III, George IV and William IV.

St George's Chapel, built between 1475 and 1528, is the scene of the Garter Service held each year. In the chapel lie Henry VI, Edward IV, Henry VIII with Jane Seymour, Charles I, as well as Edward VII and George V with their consorts. Queen Victoria and Prince Albert are buried in the green-domed mausoleum at Frogmore in the Home Park, while Edward VIII, later Duke of Windsor, lies in the royal cemetery adjoining the mausoleum. In 2002 Her Majesty Queen Elizabeth the Queen Mother was laid to rest in the chapel alongside her husband, George VI, and the ashes of her younger daughter, Princess Margaret.

On 20 November 1992, fire broke out in the Queen's Private Chapel, spreading rapidly and gutting the Chapel, the State Dining Room and the Crimson Drawing Room. The ceilings of St George's Hall and the Grand Dining Room were also destroyed. Restoration work was completed over the next five years; most rooms were restored to their original look, but the chapel was redesigned and a new ceiling created for St George's Hall.

HOUSE OF SAXE-COBURG-GOTHA

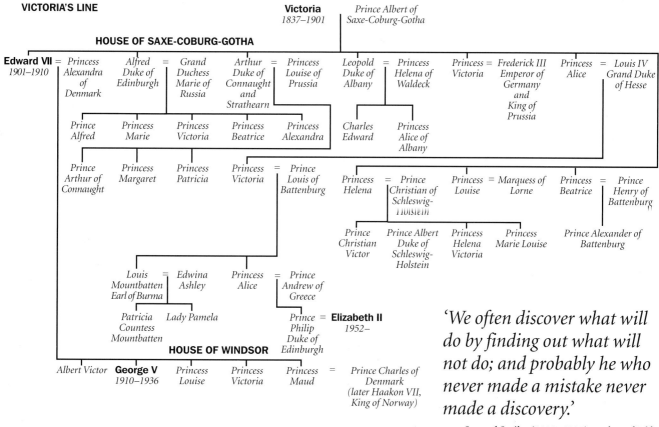

VICTORIA'S LINE

Victoria 1837–1901 — *Prince Albert of Saxe-Coburg-Gotha*

HOUSE OF SAXE-COBURG-GOTHA

Edward VII 1901–1910 = *Princess Alexandra of Denmark*

Alfred Duke of Edinburgh = *Grand Duchess Marie of Russia*

Arthur Duke of Connaught and Strathearn = *Princess Louise of Prussia*

Leopold Duke of Albany = *Princess Helena of Waldeck*

Princess Victoria = *Frederick III Emperor of Germany and King of Prussia*

Princess Alice = *Louis IV Grand Duke of Hesse*

Prince Alfred — *Princess Marie* — *Princess Victoria* — *Princess Beatrice* — *Princess Alexandra*

Charles Edward — *Princess Alice of Albany*

Prince Arthur of Connaught — *Princess Margaret* — *Princess Patricia* — *Princess Victoria* = *Prince Louis of Battenburg*

Princess Helena = *Prince Christian of Schleswig-Holstein*

Princess Louise = *Marquess of Lorne*

Princess Beatrice = *Prince Henry of Battenburg*

Prince Christian Victor — *Prince Albert Duke of Schleswig-Holstein* — *Princess Helena Victoria* — *Princess Marie Louise*

Prince Alexander of Battenburg

Louis Mountbatten Earl of Burma = *Edwina Ashley*

Princess Alice = *Prince Andrew of Greece*

Patricia Countess Mountbatten — *Lady Pamela*

Prince Philip Duke of Edinburgh = **Elizabeth II** 1952–

HOUSE OF WINDSOR

Albert Victor — **George V** 1910–1936 — *Princess Louise* — *Princess Victoria* — *Princess Maud* = *Prince Charles of Denmark (later Haakon VII, King of Norway)*

> *'We often discover what will do by finding out what will not do; and probably he who never made a mistake never made a discovery.'*
>
> Samuel Smiles (1812–1904), *author of* Self-Help, *summing up a common Victorian attitude*

ISLAND IDYLL

For Victoria and Albert, Osborne House on the Isle of Wight provided privacy, seaside holidays and domestic idyll. The queen's 'dear little home' was purchased in 1845, and rebuilt to resemble an Italian-style villa.

QUEEN VICTORIA – WHO REIGNED from her teens until her 80s – gave her name to an age of rapid and far-reaching change. Victorian Britain was a society in flux: the nation's wealth was increasing; its power and prestige reached a peak; new technology and social thinking radically altered the economy, the landscape and the everyday lives of the queen's people.

Victoria's 64-year reign was the age of the railway and steamship; of factories and coal mines; of trades unions and women's emancipation; of discoveries in science and in the wilder lands of the British Empire, whose expanding frontiers made it the greatest the world had yet seen.

This era of enterprise was locked into the 'self-help' values of the time. Charles Darwin's evolutionary theories may have rocked the foundations of science and challenged traditional beliefs, but they fitted the instincts driving a nation undergoing commercial and industrial revolution. The monarchy – unpopular and unstable in 1837 – had been strengthened by the time Victoria died in 1901, despite so many upheavals in society. Remodelled to suit the new age, the royal family had itself evolved to become a mirror of the times.

THE YOUNG VICTORIA: 1837–61

QUEEN IN COUNCIL

Queen Victoria's Privy Councillors were struck by her composure. Lord Grey commented: 'She never was in the least degree confused, embarrassed or hurried.'

SWISS COTTAGE

In 1853, Prince Albert imported a prefabricated Swiss cottage for the royal children and had it erected at Osborne. Complete with tiled kitchen and wooden dining chairs, the cottage became a playhouse where the young Princess Vicky and her sisters enter-tained their mother and father to tea.

VICTORIA WAS THE desperately desired product in 1819 of the late marriage of the Duke of Kent (George IV's brother) to Princess Victoria, widowed daughter of the Duke of Saxe-Coburg.

Fatherless from the age of eight months, Victoria was brought up in a somewhat impoverished home – for the most part away from her uncles, George IV and William IV. At 5 a.m. on the morning of 20 June 1837, the princess was woken at home in Kensington Palace to hear that she was now queen.

Determined to live up to her new role, she vowed in her journal: 'I will be good'. Her first Prime Minister (there were to be nine more) proved a perfect tutor. Lord Melbourne was aristocratic, civilized and kind: 'he knows about everything and everybody'. The two shared an instinct for people rather than systems, respect for common sense and an enjoyment of life. Victoria's coronation in 1838 was an ordeal borne bravely, and the following year came the queen's most momentous choice – of her cousin Prince Albert of Saxe-Coburg-Gotha as husband.

Victoria was ecstatic. Albert was 'quite charming and so excessively handsome, such beautiful blue eyes, and exquisite nose … '. The wedding took place on 10 February 1840 in the Chapel Royal of St James's Palace.

Albert gave stalwart support. Serious, intelligent, hard working and interested in modernizing – be it social reform, drains or the 1851 Great Exhibition – the prince was determined to do his best. Yet he was never popular; never quite belonged. Perhaps the cynical English found him too good to be true.

Victoria and Albert had nine children. When the first, 'Vicky', was born in November 1840, the attending physician was heard to say, 'Oh, Madam, it is a princess.' The exhausted Victoria replied: 'Never mind, the next will be a prince.' And it was.

A son, the Prince of Wales, arrived in November 1841. 'The Boy' was christened with his 'dear father's name', Albert Edward, but soon became known as 'Bertie'. The queen's last child, Beatrice, was born in 1857.

ROYAL FAMILY

The Winterhalter painting (1846) of stately domesticity shows the Prince of Wales (later Edward VII) beside the queen. The baby is Princess Helena, born in May 1846.

TRAVELLING IN STYLE

One of the queen's railway coaches, now on display at the National Railway Museum, York. Victoria was the first monarch to travel by train.

PRINCE ALBERT

PRINCE ALBERT'S BEE-HIVES.

SIX MILLION VISITORS

The Crystal Palace Great Exhibition of 1851 was the prince's triumph – a celebration of peace and progress through science, trade and industry. Six million people trooped through Joseph Paxton's immense glass building.

ROYAL BEEKEEPER

Albert had many interests. Here a cartoonist has fun with the prince consort and his beehives. Queen Victoria (as ever) is by his side.

FIVE DAYS AFTER VICTORIA and Albert met for the second time at Windsor Castle in 1839, the queen proposed. She wrote that she would do everything in her power 'to render the sacrifice he has made (for sacrifice in my opinion it is) as small as I can.'

On their wedding day in 1840, Victoria and Albert promised to keep no secrets from each other. Although a marriage of great contentment on both sides, for Albert the position of prince consort – a title not formally granted until 1857 – proved to be difficult.

Albert had many admirable and gentlemanly qualities. He rode, shot, fenced and danced. A man of the highest integrity, he was a devoted father who – when deskwork was done – liked nothing better than to play with his children in the palace corridors. His only disappointment was the Prince of Wales, his eldest son, quite unlike him in character and whose behaviour both parents found scandalous.

INSIDE OSBORNE

The Durbar Corridor at Osborne House contains paintings and objects with Indian associations, including portraits of Queen Victoria's Indian servants. From the corridor, guests turned into the Durbar Room, built in 1890–91 as a state banqueting hall and the first principal room at Osborne to be lit by electricity.

'It was with some emotion that I beheld Albert – who is so beautiful.'

Queen Victoria's journal, after seeing Albert, 10 October 1839

The peak of Albert's success in Britain was the 1851 Great Exhibition, held inside Joseph Paxton's brilliant Crystal Palace in Hyde Park. Its object – the betterment of mankind – was a theme Albert earnestly approved, and the enormous organization it entailed was carried out under his personal direction.

In 1845, Victoria and Albert bought Balmoral: 'a pretty little castle in the Scottish style'. Both loved the simplicity of highland life, despite the initial makeshift living arrangements – until Albert got down to 'improvements'.

But for all he did, Albert remained an outsider, the queen's husband rather than the people's prince. Overwork stressed and over-stretched him. In November 1861 he caught cold at a military inspection. Chill turned to fever, and the queen grew distraught as his condition worsened. Even in illness, the prince struggled with official business, skilfully redrafting a communication to the US government to defuse tense Anglo-US relations during the American Civil War.

Albert died on 14 December. There were stately public memorials, many smaller ones (a stone placed where he shot his last stag at Balmoral) but, in private, the queen was utterly lost. Albert's room became a shrine and her dead husband an iconic presence through the remaining 40 years of a life that would never be the same again.

THE ROYAL FAMILY

As VICTORIA AND ALBERT'S nine children grew up and married into other royal families, Britain's ageing queen became the hub of a European royal network.

1 Her Majesty Queen Victoria
2 Prince of Wales
3 Princess of Wales
4 Prince Albert Victor
5 Prince George of Wales
6 Princess Louise of Wales
7 Princess Victoria of Wales
8 Princess Maud of Wales
9 Crown Princess of Germany
10 Crown Prince of Germany
11 Prince William of Prussia
12 Princess William of Prussia

13 Prince Frederick William of Prussia
14 Hereditary Princess of Saxe-Meiningen
15 Hereditary Prince of Saxe-Meiningen
16 Princess Theodore of Saxe-Meiningen
17 Prince Henry of Prussia
18 Princess Irene of Hesse
19 Princess Victoria of Prussia
20 Princess Sophie of Prussia
21 Princess Margaret of Prussia

22 Grand Duke of Hesse
23 Princess Louis of Battenberg
24 Prince Louis of Battenberg
25 Princess Alice of Battenberg
26 Grand Duchess Elizabeth of Russia
27 Grand Duke Serge of Russia
28 Hereditary Grand Duke of Hesse
29 Princess Alix of Hesse
30 Duke of Edinburgh

REGAL MATRIARCH

A painting commissioned for Queen Victoria's 1887 Golden Jubilee shows the queen surrounded by members of this vast royal family. She was related, directly or by marriage, to eight European royal houses.

31 Duchess of Edinburgh
32 Prince Alfred of Edinburgh
33 Princess Marie of Edinburgh
34 Princess Victoria Melita of Edinburgh
35 Princess Alexandra of Edinburgh
36 Princess Beatrice of Edinburgh
37 Princess Christian of Schleswig-Holstein, Princess Helena of Great Britain and Ireland
38 Prince Christian of Schleswig-Holstein
39 Prince Christian Victor of Schleswig-Holstein
40 Prince Albert of Schleswig-Holstein
41 Princess Victoria of Schleswig-Holstein
42 Princess Louise of Schleswig-Holstein
43 Princess Louise, Marchioness of Lorne
44 Marquess of Lorne
45 Duke of Connaught
46 Duchess of Connaught
47 Princess Margaret of Connaught
48 Prince Arthur of Connaught
49 Princess Victoria Beatrice Patricia of Connaught
50 Duchess of Albany
51 Princess Alice of Albany
52 Prince Charles Edward, Duke of Albany
53 Princess Beatrice, Princess Henry of Battenberg
54 Prince Henry of Battenberg
55 Prince Alexander Albert of Battenberg

111

A QUEEN IN MOURNING: 1861–1901

TWO DAYS AFTER ALBERT'S DEATH, Victoria wrote to her eldest daughter Princess Victoria in Germany. 'My darling Angel's child – Our firstborn. God's will be done.'

~

Prince Albert's loss was a shattering blow. Prolonged mourning was expected, but Victoria took it to extremes that alarmed the government. Not until the late 1870s did she resume anything like a normal public life.

~

People's sympathy turned to impatience, even resentment, since the grieving queen would not let the Prince of Wales take on the ceremonial face of monarchy while she stayed hidden away, swathed in widow's black, gazing sorrowfully at the bust of dear, departed Albert.

~

Criticism of the queen was not completely justified, since she never stopped working on state papers, though ministers found her difficult and sometimes inaccessible. Of her two most illustrious Prime Ministers, she much preferred Disraeli, who made her laugh and believed in imperial glory. Gladstone never raised a royal smile. 'He speaks to me as if I was a public meeting,' the queen complained.

THE FATHERLESS FAMILY

A photograph of Queen Victoria taken at Windsor Castle in 1862; with the queen are Princess Victoria (standing), Princess Alice and Prince Alfred.

That the queen became reclusive is true. That she found solace in the companionship of servants such as John Brown is also true. Otherwise she found consolation in children and grandchildren – though not the Prince of Wales. Delighted to be named Empress of India in 1876, she sent comforts to the troops during the Boer Wars, and was exhilarated though surprised by cheering crowds celebrating her Golden (1887) and Diamond (1897) Jubilees. In 1896 she became the longest reigning European sovereign – still taking an interest in such new developments as the telephone, car and moving-picture camera.

Victoria's last weeks were spent at her beloved holiday home, Osborne, on the Isle of Wight. There over Christmas 1900 she weakened, dying peacefully on the evening of 22 January 1901 among her family and on the arm of the German Kaiser, her grandson. Her last word was 'Bertie,' the eldest son who was finally to become king.

'A PRETTY LITTLE CASTLE'

So Queen Victoria described Balmoral, her 'dear paradise' on the banks of the River Dee. She loved the romance of the Scottish Highlands and liked talking to the people – 'so simple and straightforward'. Balmoral was full of memories of Albert, and she spent more and more time there after his death.

MEMORIALS TO ALBERT

The Royal Albert Hall (1867–71) in London (left) was designed by Francis Fowke. The Albert Memorial (1863–76) across the road was the work of Giles Gilbert Scott. This twice life-sized gilt-bronze statue shows Albert holding a catalogue of the Great Exhibition.

EDWARD VII (1901–10)

VICTORIA'S FUNERAL

People who saw Queen Victoria's funeral never forgot it. Black drapes were banished (on the queen's instructions) in favour of white and gold. Victoria's last public journey was made through packed, silent streets, escorted by troops from around the empire. The Kaiser had measured her for her coffin; her sons 'Bertie' (now King Edward VII) and Prince Arthur lifted her into it. She wore her wedding veil, with spring flowers laid on her white dress.

After the lying-in-state at Osborne House, the coffin was moved to the royal yacht *Alberta* for its journey to the mainland and then by train to London's Victoria station. All along the route, people stood bare-headed, many in tears. A gun carriage took the coffin to Paddington for the second train journey to Windsor. From the park, a salute of 81 guns boomed, one for each year of the queen's life. A brief service in St George's Chapel (a place she had never liked) was followed by a second lying-in-state in the Albert Memorial Chapel. The queen was laid to rest, beside Prince Albert, on 4 February in the mausoleum. Snow began to fall as the family mourners dispersed.

EDWARD VII ('BERTIE' to his family) was born in 1841 and had to wait almost 60 years to become king. Given little to do during this long apprenticeship, he chose – to the alarm of his well-intentioned parents Victoria and Albert – the card-tables of fashionable society rather than the desk of diligent duty.

The smartest, richest homes in Britain welcomed the Prince of Wales for weekend parties, and while his amatory adventures were open society secrets, there were no tabloid newspapers headlining 'kiss and tell' stories. His marriage to Princess Alexandra of Denmark in 1863 was publicly affectionate and 'proper', however, and the prince was a kindly father.

WINDSOR MOURNING
Queen Victoria's funeral procession passes through Windsor, February 1901.

Edward VII proved a more able monarch than many had expected. Politically conservative, befitting a country gentleman who loved shooting and horse racing (his horses winning the Derby three times), he also enjoyed the London theatre. His reign saw Britain's first old-age pensions and National Insurance schemes, but also the arms race that led to the First World War.

Stately Edward fitted the role of imperial monarch, and he helped stiffen the Entente Cordiale with France, earning approval from a music-hall song ('There'll be no war, as long as there's a king like good King Edward') but outraging the Kaiser. Though he failed to restrain his German nephew's ambitions, Edward earned people's affections and the title 'Peacemaker'. Edward VII died, on 6 May 1910, four years before the start of the war he had worked hard to prevent.

Queen Victoria at the christening in 1894 of Edward, later Edward VIII and Duke of Windsor. To the right is his grandfather, the Prince of Wales (the future Edward VII); to the left his father, the Duke of York (later George V).

'We are all socialists nowadays.'

The future Edward VII addressing a Mansion House audience in 1895

SANDRINGHAM HOUSE

In 1862 the Prince of Wales bought an estate in Norfolk, and in 1867–70 a house was built there for him. Sandringham remains a favourite royal home.

HOUSE OF WINDSOR

HOUSE OF WINDSOR

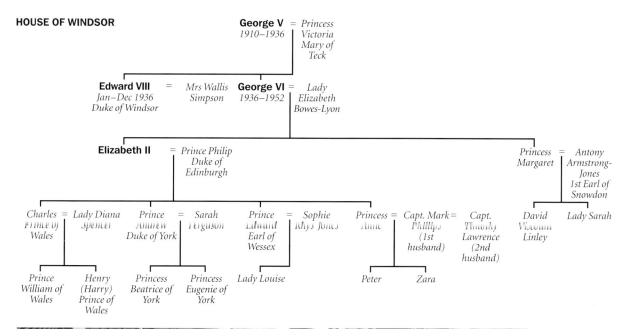

George V = *Princess Victoria Mary of Teck*
1910–1936

Edward VIII = *Mrs Wallis Simpson*
Jan–Dec 1936
Duke of Windsor

George VI = *Lady Elizabeth Bowes-Lyon*
1936–1952

Elizabeth II = *Prince Philip Duke of Edinburgh*

Princess Margaret = *Antony Armstrong-Jones 1st Earl of Snowdon*

Charles = *Lady Diana Spencer*
Prince of Wales

Prince Andrew = *Sarah Ferguson*
Duke of York

Prince Edward = *Sophie Rhys-Jones*
Earl of Wessex

Princess Anne = *Capt. Mark Phillips (1st husband)* = *Capt. Timothy Lawrence (2nd husband)*

David Viscount Linley   *Lady Sarah*

Prince William of Wales   *Henry (Harry) Prince of Wales*

Princess Beatrice of York   *Princess Eugenie of York*

Lady Louise

Peter   *Zara*

THANKSGIVING IN 1935

The Royal Family enter St Paul's Cathedral for the Silver Jubilee Service of Thanksgiving, 1935. Left to right are the Princesses Elizabeth and Margaret with the Duke and Duchess of York; the Prince of Wales; George V and Queen Mary.

ROYAL CENTREPIECE

Buckingham Palace is the focus for royal public appearances, as well as for ceremonies, banquets, receptions and investitures. The first sovereign to live here was Queen Victoria, for whose growing family the East Front (now photographed by myriads of tourists) was added between 1847–53.

WHEN QUEEN VICTORIA DIED in 1901, she left three generations of heirs. They, it was expected, would reign as monarchs of the House of Saxe-Coburg-Gotha. In fact, the name survived only 16 years. In 1917, King George V announced that the name was no more. The rising horrors of the First World War had filled a reservoir of anti-German feeling, and the royal family's German name was no longer politically correct. Henceforth the House of Windsor would reign.

The Windsor dynasty survived three turbulent decades spanning the Great War, Communist revolution, the Wall Street Crash, the Depression and the rise of fascism. It was shaken by the abdication crisis of 1936, after which the title Duke of Windsor was created for the former king, Edward VIII. His brother, King George VI, unexpectedly thrust onto the throne, proved equal to a task made more onerous by the perils of the Second World War.

Following the period of post-war austerity, the accession of George VI's daughter Elizabeth II in 1952 was greeted with enthusiasm. Yet this was to be no new romantic Elizabethan age. An era of questioning, intrusive mass media exposed the monarchy to scrutiny unthinkable in earlier generations. Under this spotlight, in a changing Britain, the monarchy continues to evolve within the society it represents – something it has achieved successfully for over a thousand years.

GEORGE V (1910–36)

EDWARD VII'S ELDEST SON Albert died at the age of 28, and so it was his second son, George, who followed him as king. George had learned the navy's traditions of duty and loyalty. Blue-eyed, blunt, and unafraid to express an opinion on things he did not care for, George was more interested in guns and boats than intellectual pursuits. In 1893 he was married to Princess Victoria Mary of Teck, the intended bride of his elder brother.

George V's reign was overshadowed by the First World War (1914–18), troubles in Ireland and the Russian revolution that removed Tsar Nicholas, a relative who shared a marked likeness to the king.

IMPERIAL MONARCH

George V's manner and bearing suited his role as monarch to the British Empire, even at a time when that empire was evolving into the new, less coherent organization of the Commonwealth.

QUEEN MARY

Here painted by C.S. Jagger, Queen Mary was admired for her dignity and devotion to duty, qualities she passed on to her granddaughter Elizabeth.

'The most perfect present that anyone could receive.'

Queen Mary, on the royal dolls' house

QUEEN MARY'S DOLLS' HOUSE

Probably the most magnificently complete dolls' house in the world is Queen Mary's, on display at Windsor Castle. Created both as a gift to the king's consort and to raise funds for charity, the house first went on public view at the British Empire Exhibition of 1924, and was moved to Windsor the following year.

Perfect to the smallest detail, the house was built under the direction of the architect Sir Edwin Lutyens to the scale of one-twelfth normal size. It has over 40 rooms, and is a microcosm of 1920s life, mingling the old and new. The house has electric light, two lifts, hot and cold water plumbing, a miniature vacuum cleaner and a coal-burning kitchen range. Externally the house represents a mansion in the classical tradition. It has gardens designed by Gertrude Jekyll, with metal flowers (and even tiny snails), a library and specially created paintings. The dining room has a table measuring 50 centimetres (20 inches) when extended and is set for 14 places. The largest room is the saloon, in which there are two thrones, a grand piano and a silk wall-covering woven to the incredible scale of 120 threads to the inch.

The monarch performed his role as national figurehead with energy and dignity. In 1911 he became the first British emperor to visit India. During the war he frequently visited the Western Front, besides touring factories and hospitals at home. To placate anti-German feeling, he gave up the family name. In 1921 he inaugurated the Parliament of Northern Ireland and in 1924 opened the British Empire Exhibition at Wembley. The same year saw the election of Britain's first Labour government, led by Ramsay MacDonald.

Following a virus infection in 1929, the king's health was less robust – not that he cared much for medical opinion. The 'Sailor King' lived out his last years as a constitutional monarch in the fast-changing world of the 1930s – uncertain times in which the throne's popularity and people's affection for the monarch steadily grew. In 1932 King George made the first royal Christmas radio broadcast, and in 1935 his Silver Jubilee generated real popular affection – somewhat to the king's surprise. He died at Sandringham, his Norfolk home, in January 1936.

WONDERS REVEALED

An outer shell lifts to show the interior of Queen Mary's dolls' house. Its garage stores six cars, including a tiny Rolls-Royce Silver Ghost.

MASTERWORKS IN MINIATURE

A cricket bat from the dolls' house, shown beside a full-size ball.

EDWARD VIII AND GEORGE VI: 1936–52

EDWARD VIII (1936)

EDWARD, PRINCE OF WALES, eldest son of George V and Queen Mary, was known to the family as 'David'. Charming and informal, he was a popular prince, touring Britain and the empire, fond of golf, tennis, parties and dancing. Wanting to serve in the First World War, he was kept away from the front line lest he be killed or, worse, captured. Later, he was banned from riding in steeplechases and learning to fly.

The prince found such restraints irksome, while his parents were upset by his refusal to marry and settle down. When the prince's choice fell on a twice-divorced American, Mrs Wallis Simpson, constitutional problems arose. Never steady or strong of will, the prince had to decide between Mrs Simpson and the Crown, which passed to him in 1936 on the death of his father George V. In the event, Edward VIII became the only British sovereign to resign the throne of his own will.

He abdicated on 10 December, broadcasting a memorable farewell message by radio, and left the country to marry Mrs Simpson in France. He was made Duke of Windsor and lived abroad, maintaining friendly if distant links with his relatives until his death in 1972.

FOREVER THE PRINCE OF WALES

Edward VIII, handsome and popular in youth, was never crowned. After the abdication, he took no significant part in British public life.

GEORGE VI (1936–52)

George V's second son Albert ('Bertie') was a year younger than the Prince of Wales. Naturally shy, and with a stammer that – until partially mastered – made public speaking an ordeal, the Duke of York was happiest as a naval officer and family man. He fought at the Battle of Jutland in 1916, was the first royal family member to fly a plane, and enjoyed a happy married life with Elizabeth Bowes-Lyon and their two daughters, Elizabeth (born 1926) and Margaret (born 1930).

The abdication crisis of 1936 tossed 'Bertie' into the limelight and onto the throne. He shouldered the unexpected and unwanted burden bravely, especially during the Second World War. For wartime Britain and its empire, George VI and Queen Elizabeth became symbols of quiet defiance. They stayed in London during the Blitz, touring bombed districts and identifying the royal family with the national war effort. Prime Minister Winston Churchill found in the king a trusted ally.

The king, never robust, saw his daughter Elizabeth marry in 1947 but became ill the following year. In 1951 he opened the Festival of Britain, and doctors diagnosed his illness as lung cancer. Although an operation appeared to be successful, the king died suddenly in his sleep after a day's shooting at Sandringham on 6 February 1952.

'Something must be done.'

Edward, Prince of Wales, shocked by the plight of the unemployed in South Wales

'I'm glad we've been bombed. It makes me feel we can look the East End in the face.'

Queen Elizabeth in 1940, after Buckingham Palace had been hit by a German daylight raid

AT WAR AGAIN

On 3 September 1939, George VI wrote in his diary: 'Today we are at War again, and I am no longer a midshipman in the Royal Navy' – a reference to his youth at the outbreak of the First World War in 1914. Speaking that evening to his people by radio, the king said: **'We can only do the right as we see the right and reverently commit our cause to God.'**

ROYAL BOMBSHELL

King George VI and Queen Elizabeth survey the damage to their London home on the morning of 10 September 1940. Five days later, another bomb landed on the palace.

A PUBLIC CORONATION

George VI's coronation took place in 1937, on the date fixed for the crowning of his older brother. It was the first coronation to be broadcast on radio.

ELIZABETH II (1952–)

PRINCESS ELIZABETH ALEXANDRA MARY was born at 17 Bruton Street, London on 21 April 1926. A happy childhood was spent with her parents, the Duke and Duchess of York, and younger sister Margaret Rose. Present at her parents' coronation in 1937, at the age of 14 she broadcast to the children of the empire.

Educated at home, in the Second World War she joined the Auxiliary Transport Service (ATS). In 1947 she visited South Africa, celebrating her 21st birthday there and broadcasting a moving promise to dedicate herself to the empire's service. In July came her engagement to Philip Mountbatten, formerly Prince Philip of Greece and Denmark, who had seen wartime service in the Royal Navy. The two were married on 20 November 1947.

Their first child, Prince Charles, was born in 1948, and Princess Anne in 1950. Just two years later, news of George VI's death came during Princess Elizabeth's visit to Kenya. A wave of optimism enveloped the new queen, amid expectations of 'a new Elizabethan age'. But her reign, though long, has not always been as happy and glorious as the coronation mood of 1953 suggested. That coronation was the last truly imperial event in British history. It was also the first to be televised.

The Queen is now the longest reigning British monarch since Queen Victoria. Her Silver (1977) and Golden (2002) Jubilees were marked by parties and

'The things which I have here before promised, I will perform and keep. So help me God.'

From the Coronation Oath

CORONATION DAY

On 2 June 1953 Elizabeth was crowned 'Elizabeth the Second, by the Grace of God, of Great Britain and Northern Ireland and of her other Realms and Territories, Queen, Head of the Commonwealth, Defender of the Faith.'

' … an entirely new conception built on the highest qualities of the spirit of man: friendship, loyalty and the desire for freedom and peace.'

The Queen on the Commonwealth

parades that helped restore the image of a royal family battered by intrusive media in an age determined to ditch deference. Tabloid 'hounding', tempered somewhat after Princess Diana's death in 1997, included prolonged dissection of the monarchy's role, cost and size, and extensive coverage of young family members' marital breakdowns.

The monarchy has reacted to changing events: a more 'presidential' style of premiership; devolution in Scotland and Wales; the shift from Commonwealth to European Union. It has become less aloof. Buckingham Palace opened to the public to fund restoration work on fire-damaged Windsor Castle. The royal yacht went into retirement. The Queen's decision to pay income tax and fund family members is another sign of changing times. Although the Queen lost both her mother (at the age of 101) and her sister in 2002, the Duke of Edinburgh – 'my rock' – remained at her side to carry out the role of royal consort with humour and energy. Queen Elizabeth II stated clearly from the start that her service would be lifelong. Her dedication and example have ensured that the ancient Crown of these islands carries into the 21st century the inspirational echoes of over a thousand years of history.

BALCONY SCENE

The balcony at Buckingham Palace, often the setting for national events, as the newly-crowned Queen appears before crowds gathered to wave, cheer, take photos – and remember.

GOLDEN JUBILEE 2002

A youthful escort surrounds the Queen on her 50th anniversary walkabout in London.

A LIFETIME'S SERVICE

'I declare before you all that my whole life, whether it be long or short, shall be devoted to your service.' These words, spoken on her 21st birthday, sum up the Queen's attitude to her position. This most travelled of all monarchs (she has visited over 100 countries and been seen by more people than all her ancestors put together) has always seen being sovereign as a lifetime commitment.

INTO THE FUTURE

ROYAL SALUTE

The Queen takes the salute, as ever on show and under the watchful gaze of the media and the people.

ELIZABETH II HAS REIGNED in a world moving swiftly through political shifts, cultural change and technological advances. Traditional institutions of law, religion and politics have suffered loss of esteem, but the Queen has remained steadfast and unwavering, a focus of stability. Her devotion to duty has won respect and admiration not only in Britain but also throughout the Commonwealth and wider world.

The Queen carries out a demanding round of engagements. At heart a countrywoman, 'happiest with dogs and horses', she moves serenely through the great state events – the Opening of Parliament, Trooping the Colour, the Cenotaph Ceremony of Remembrance. The pageantry of these occasions – also enjoyed and admired by visitors to Britain – means that 'putting on a show' is part of the modern monarchy's public relations activities. Unique treasures such as the crown jewels and golden State Coach inspire awe even in an age of special effects and virtual reality.

The Queen's children have pursued their own lives and interests. Charles, Prince of Wales (born 14 November 1948) served in the Royal Navy and has undertaken a wide range of public duties, many reflecting his personal interests. Charles married Lady Diana Spencer on 29 July 1981. Diana blossomed from a shy teenager into an international celebrity, but what had at first seemed a fairy-tale romance ended in

public breakdown, acrimony and divorce. Diana's death in a Paris car crash (31 August 1997) released a surge of public emotion that threatened to overwhelm the dignity and traditional formality of the monarchy.

Princess Anne's marriage to Captain Mark Phillips also ended in divorce; she later became the wife of naval officer Timothy Lawrence. Prince Andrew, Duke of York, served as a helicopter pilot in the Falklands War (1982) during his naval career. His marriage to Sarah Ferguson also ended, though amicably. The Queen's youngest son, Prince Edward, Earl of Wessex, worked for a while in media production and is married to Sophie Rhys-Jones.

The modern media is hungry for 'royal stories'. The Prince of Wales suffered a 'bad press' in some quarters during the break-up of his marriage, while Diana, the 'people's princess', was given superstar treatment in the media, being seen by some as young and 'caring' in contrast to an older tradition of royal 'separateness'.

The Queen and Prince Charles showed resilience in surmounting these problems. Charles's concern for giving practical help was shown by setting up the Prince's Trust, while willingness to accept change in a changing nation earned him respect, as did his evident devotion to his two sons, Prince William (born 21 June 1982) and Prince Harry (born 15 September 1984).

And so the royal line runs on, as it has for many generations, and through many triumphs and disasters. The monarchy continues to be a strong thread in the fabric of national life, its powers reduced, its pageantry more symbolic, but its magic at times hardly any the less diminished.

STATE OCCASION
The State Opening of Parliament features a carriage procession, ceremonial robes, and the Queen's Speech – which is written for her by the government of the day. The Queen's role within the constitution is largely symbolic, but pivotal.

INDEX